In THE ART OF BEING HUMAN, *Fr. McNamara tells us that:*

Giving honor and glory to God is the purpose of all life. Humans give glory to God by being human—by being as human as possible.

On that day that we become as perfectly human as we can in this world, then we shall be saints. Live saints, not dead saints. If, here and now, we are not saints, it is only because we are not human enough. I think the best definition of a saint is: a whole man—holy. That is why it is true to say that if a man does not become a saint he is a failure.

Now, what is it that distinguishes us from every other animal in the world and really makes us human? It is the spiritual powers of knowing and loving. When these powers are fully exercised and satisfied, then we are completely humanized. But God is the only object that can fully exercise and satisfy the human capacity for knowledge and love. Therefore, it is loving knowledge of God and His creation that makes a saint; not flight from the world, multiplication of devotions, or even moral rectitude.

The sanctifying process is a humanizing process. It is the progressive enlightenment of the mind and enlargement of the heart. It is to know God so well that you fall in love with Him—and once you know Him you've got to love Him.

To emphasize the human element in the process of sanctification is not to ignore the divine; to save the value of the creature is not to lose the infinitely greater value of the Creator: as though the *other* from Him were *apart* from Him, as though He had to compete with other forces and therefore demand that we love nothing but Him. It's that false "either-or" principle that keeps cropping up in spiritual writings. To hold creatures cheap, St. Thomas remarks, is to slight divine power. We must frown on nothing except our sins.

This is Father McNamara's approach to how any one of us can accomplish THE ART OF BEING HUMAN.

THE ART OF
BEING HUMAN

WILLIAM McNAMARA, O.C.D.

ECHO BOOKS

A DIVISION OF DOUBLEDAY & COMPANY, INC.
GARDEN CITY, NEW YORK

Echo Books edition published October 1967 by special arrangement with the Bruce Publishing Company

Nihil obstat: Reverend John Prah, o.c.d., *Censor ordinis*
Reverend Kenneth Stansky, o.c.d., *Censor ordinis*
Imprimi potest: Very Reverend Christopher Latimer, o.c.d., *Provincial*

Nihil obstat: John A. Schulien, s.t.d., *Censor librorum*
Imprimatur: William E. Cousins, Archbishop of Milwaukee
July 17, 1962

To the really *human* people I have met
who have enriched my life

Thanks to *Ave Maria* and *Today* magazines for permission to utilize and rewrite some material that originally appeared in those publications.

CONTENTS

INTRODUCTION

Paradise is for St. Thomas the culmination and fulfillment of what is here begun. To see God through the Beatific Vision is heaven; to see Him as through a cloudy glass is to begin heaven on earth. One of the older and eminent writers of the Church, Boethius, defined heaven as "the state which is perfect in the assemblage of all good things."

The aim of Christian humanism is to come as close as possible to the realization of this goal here on earth. Our life in the world is not merely a trial discontinuous and unrelated to the life of heaven. Heaven is the *crowning point* of beatitude—perfect vision, joy, happiness. But that is the *end* of beatitude (the final, glorious, everlasting, unfading phase) not the beginning. "I have come that you may have life and have it more abundantly," here and now, despite the meanness and the squalor all around you, and the weakness within you. That is the *beginning* of beatitude.

So man must live now—fully, richly, divinely. Toward that end this book was written. It deals with the few basic things man needs for his wholeness—his holiness.

You can call this approach Christian humanism, the doctrine which urges man to find in the integral acceptance of Christianity the highest accomplishment of his humanity.

Christian piety all too often has taken the form of withdrawal from the world and from men, a sort of dignified, spiritual egotism, an indifference to the suffering of the world and man, a cultivation of a plot of spiritual ground in the suburbs of reality. Such piety is emasculated, starved of Christian love and mercy. It is frigid, unreal, devoid of human warmth.

Men, today, are rising in protest against this selfish form of piety. Against their protest only a newborn, vigorous, selfless piety can stand. Our piety must be full of care and concern for our fellowman, for his survival and enrichment, and for the improvement of his world. This endeavor involves essentially spiritual activity. To look after my own material welfare may, indeed, be a material question; but to look after my neighbor, even his material welfare, is a spiritual question.

Péguy went to the heart of the matter when he wrote that depreciation of the temporal, of nature, of the world is not enough to raise one to the eternal, or to grace or to God. Lack of sufficient courage to be worldly does not make one unworldly. Lack of love for man does not mean love of God.

And yet Jesus Christ was a man.

Thinking out the problems of today in terms of positive, alert Christian humanism does not mean that we are going "all the way" with the spirit or the pattern of technology in the ridiculous fear of appearing reactionary, and not up-to-date. We must, in fact, absolutely resist the temptation of making technology the pattern of human life. We must steadfastly restrict the role of technology to its limited and proper domain. We must safeguard all the higher, nobler spheres of human life from being invaded by the spirit of technology.

We must protect and emphasize, perhaps more than anything else, the supreme human activity: contemplation.

To grant to contemplation a greater role is not only a way of counteracting the trend toward excessive technology; it is necessary in itself as the highest and deepest actualization of personality, as well as the indispensable source of all deep and effective forms of activity, whether they be moral, philosophical, or artistic. Activity without contemplation is blind.

You can reduce this whole book to twelve very simple principles of Christian humanism. I shall list them here:

1. The final goal of man is transcendent, supernatural; but it is a goal of man, a fulfillment of his nature.

2. Grace does not destroy nature, it perfects it. It does not overlay it; it permeates and transfigures the whole of it.

3. The mission of Christ is always the same: "to save that which perished." And that which perished was not only a soul but the whole man, as well as the material universe in which context all men are to be saved.

4. Christ is the origin and source as well as the supreme instance of humanism. Apart from Him there is no human perfection. Man is not perfectly human until he is partly divine. This divinization of man through grace is the necessary, obligatory goal of all humans and, therefore, the one essential business of any form of humanism.

5. Ever since the Incarnation no man is permitted to scorn or disregard anything human or natural. Human wholeness is holiness.

6. No man may take care of his own soul and let the world go hang. No man becomes perfect by seeking perfection directly; it is a by-product of his human effort to glorify God by human work well done.

7. Man should not flee from the world to be free of it; he should enter into it to transform it; he should not scorn the secular, he should integrate it with the spiritual; he should not aim at rejection but at consecration.

8. Man must not hate the world; he must turn toward it with redemptive healing love. He must expend himself with toil, pain, the tears and sweat of mental and manual labor toward the transformation and perfection of the world.

9. Man must have a "long view" of reality, not a timid and limited vision. The danger of technical progress, involving, as it often does, dehumanizing conditions of work, ought not to lead man to despair, but to a deeper wisdom and a more intelligent control of things.

10. Human perfection means freedom. And there is no freedom without detachment—detachment from all that is not God. But detachment is not a flight from the world, nor a disinclination to creatures, nor a safe noncommittalism. It is, rather, a daring, solicitous, warmhearted, unselfish love of everything. Detachment does not mean that you love nothing but God; it means that you love all in God—the manifold in the One. It does not mean that you learn to love creatures less and less, it means that you learn to love them more and more—but selflessly, as part of your vast, undivided love of God.

11. The spirit of poverty (detachment) is not easily come by. It demands a reasonable, generous program of mortifica-

tion as well as periodic withdrawals into solitude. It also involves the readiness of man to sacrifice himself and his temporal works to the glory of God. That God may, indeed, require of him such a sacrifice of temporal achievements inspires even greater energy and devotion toward temporal affairs. Should he be asked to lay his gift on the sacrificial altar it will be the most perfect his hands can offer.

12. A man must base his life upon principles of sanctity, not principles of safety. Dangerous territory must be traversed while the delicate Christian balance is preserved.

THE ART OF
BEING HUMAN

1 · BECOMING HUMAN

Since this book is about becoming human, I could hardly begin with a more appropriate question than: What is the purpose of human life?

It is a common question; so common it is barely noticed; hardly ever answered; almost never faced squarely and seriously. The fact is that most people have the wrong idea of the purpose of life. You ask ten men this basic question and nine of them will say: "The purpose of life is to save my soul." And they'll back it up with dozens of catechisms.

But it's wrong. I don't say it's heretical. It is certainly not, strictly speaking, a theological error. It has, in fact, some good but very limited, partial theological sense. However, it is the psychological ramifications of such an answer in the actual life of a real human being that are distressing.

Just imagine what would happen, for instance, if you really believed that the first and foremost purpose of life was to save your own soul, and you set out seriously to do it. All your thoughts, desires, and actions, even your service to your neighbor, even your lovemaking, would be, primarily, for your own sake. You see what is happening? You are becoming an egotistic horror; and in the name of religion. You are losing your capacity to judge things objectively, to respond to value other than your own, to act selflessly, to love. You come to the aid of your hungry, needy neighbor not because he is good, a living witness of Christ, an image of God; but rather for what you get out of this service, namely, merit, growth in grace, assurance of your own salvation.

There are many pious people who stifle their love and spoil their lives by an inordinate desire to save their own souls. You've got to save your soul. This is vastly important: "What doth it profit a man to gain the whole world if he loses his own soul?" But the point is: you save your soul best, without any unwholesome, un-Christian psychological effects, by setting out, first of all, to fulfill the purpose of life.

What is it, then, if not the salvation of one's soul? Well, you can't improve on the Word of God. And if you read the Gospel you will notice that whenever our Lord speaks of the purpose of life it is never in terms of "getting" anything: moral improvement, perfection, or salvation. It is always in terms of "giving"—*giving honor and glory to God.* That is the purpose of life. The by-product of zest and zeal for God's glory is perfection, holiness, and, certainly, salvation.

That is what our Lord meant when He said that we must seek first His kingdom, and everything else would unfold inevitably, graciously. And when He said that we must lose our lives in order to save them, He was talking about the same thing.

In other words, we must be so concerned about God and His kingdom, His glory, His will, that we come very close to forgetting about ourselves. We must be so taken up with our Father's business, that we would never think of setting up a pokey little business of our own. And so our petty little problems get swallowed up in the unrelenting, consuming pursuit of God's honor and glory.

Giving honor and glory to God is the purpose of all life—vegetable and animal as well as human. Trees give glory to God by being good, decent trees. Dogs give glory to God by being as doggy as possible. Humans give glory to God by being human—by being as human as possible.

On that day that we become as perfectly human as we can in this world, then we shall be saints. Live saints, not dead saints; human saints, not odd, sour-faced, or inhuman saints. If, here and now, we are not saints, it is only because we are not human enough. I think the best definition of a saint is: a whole man—holy. That is why it is true to say that if a man does not become a saint he is a failure.

Now, what is it that distinguishes us from every other animal in the world and really makes us human? It is the spiritual powers of knowing and loving. When these powers are fully exercised and satisfied, then we are completely humanized. But God is the only object that can fully exercise and satisfy the human capacity for knowledge and love. Therefore, it is loving knowledge of God and His creation

that makes a saint; not flight from the world, multiplication
of devotions, or even moral rectitude.

The sanctifying process is a humanizing process. It is the
progressive enlightenment of the mind and enlargement of
the heart. It is to know God so well that you fall in love with
Him—and once you know Him you've got to love Him: He
is so infinitely lovable—and it is this positive, outgoing, unselfish love that drives you to avoid evil and practice virtue,
and do penance. But above all, it makes you human—kind,
joyous, enthusiastic, adventurous, uproariously happy, re-
lentlessly apostolic.

To emphasize the human element in the process of sanctification is not to ignore the divine; to save the value of the
creature is not to lose the infinitely greater value of the Creator: as though the *other* from Him were *apart* from Him,
as though He had to compete with other forces and therefore demand that we love nothing but Him. It's that false
"either-or" principle that keeps cropping up in spiritual writings. To hold creatures cheap, St. Thomas remarks, is to
slight divine power. We must frown on nothing except our
sins.

Charity is not just the soul's response to the breath of the
Spirit. It is rather the response of the whole man to the
touch of the triune personal love of God (grace). We are
called into lasting friendship with God, and to make us purely
instruments ruling us out as lovers, St. Thomas boldly says,
does not enhance but diminishes the dignity of charity. You
will not find in St. Thomas any kinship with those who say
that grace works best when everything congenial to us has
been pumped out. Nature abhors a vacuum, and so does
supernature. Grace does not dwell, like a lonely, lofty light,
in the attic of the personality. It is not limited even to what
is technically spiritual. It suffuses and permeates the whole
person, transfigures the whole man. St. Thomas, for instance,
does not regard the infused virtues of fortitude and temper-
ance as qualities of our higher selves or habits of willpower,
but rather as transfigurations of emotion: fortitude is a
temper restrained or fired according to circumstances; tem-
perance is passion and pleasure controlled but unmitigated.

Man is at heart created and conserved by divine power, and his activity is motored and energized by that same power which wells up in him like a living, superabundant fountain of life divinizing him at every level, and expanding through every part of his organic personality.

It is this merging of the natural and the supernatural that brings us to the affirmation of the second big point of this first chapter, and the point is: *you cannot become perfectly human until you are partly divine.*

In other words, the humanizing process is from beginning to end a divinizing process—a suffering of divine things, a transformation into Christ, a life dominated by the indwelling Spirit. This is the mystical life. The whole man must, then, be a mystic.

A mystic is one who knows God by experience. All of the Apostles were mystics. John, the beloved disciple, opens up his first epistle with a clear, outspoken admission of this fundamental fact.

We proclaim what was from the beginning, what we have heard, what we have seen with our own eyes, what we have gazed upon, and what we have embraced with our own hands. I refer to the Word who is and who imparts life. Indeed, this Life has manifested himself. We ourselves have seen and testify and proclaim that Eternal Life which was with the Father and has manifested himself. To you we proclaim what we have seen and heard, that you may share our treasure with us. That treasure is union with the Father and his Son, Jesus Christ. I write this to you that we may have joy in the fullest measure (1 Jn 1:1–4).

John, the beloved disciple, has given his witness. What he once touched and tasted and handled, that he has declared unto us. It was the shining, the epiphany of God the Father which he and the Twelve had discovered tabernacled close at their side in the body of Christ. "We saw his Glory, the glory as of God himself."

The Disciple's first encounter was the day he saw Jesus coming toward him and a wonderful word broke from the Baptist: "Behold, the Lamb of God." The words fascinated, haunted him, and when, on the following day, John uttered

them again, three of them at least could not rest; their hearts
burned to know more.

So two of them, and John the beloved who tells the story,
followed Him. Now that He, the stranger, found them following, He turned and spoke. For the first time, then, He
looked upon them with that look which again and again had
the power to draw a soul, by one glance, out of the night of
sin into the life of eternal light. And so they heard His voice
—that voice which by its cry could raise the dead. "Whom
seek ye?" That was all. And they hardly knew what to say
—only they must see Him, must go with Him; and they stam-
mered: "Rabbi, where dwellest thou?" And He said: "Come
and see."

They went and saw. So intense is the Apostle's memory
of that personal encounter that he can never forget the very
hour of the day. It was just ten o'clock when he got to the
house. They stayed with Him long enough to know, by experience, who He was.

This religious experience of the Apostles is a basic, simple
form of what we call mysticism. The typical mystic is the
person who has a certain firsthand experience and knowledge
of God through love. This is quite different from knowledge
by hearsay or cold, detached study. It is what breathes
eternal life into the latter forms of abstract knowledge. "And
this is eternal life that you may know God, and Jesus Christ
whom he has sent."

We are prone in our thinking to limit the modes of God's
action in people to forms familiar to us; hence we tend to
restrict unduly the number of contemplatives. There is a
different form not only for each great saint, but for each person, even the most ordinary.

This experience of God may come in many ways and
under many symbolic disguises. It may be steady or fleeting, dim or intense. But insofar as it is direct and intuitive it
is always a mystical experience.

Experience is a difficult term to tie down with the threads
of definition or description. The word which seems to get
closest to the heart of things is *awareness*: the subjective reaction to some objective reality which is perceived in some

way by the subject. This awareness can be conscious and unconscious; and that is what makes the difference between a saint who is a mystic and one who isn't; but the awareness of God possessed in common by both is in each case genuinely, essentially mystical.

This awareness is not simply an intellectual recognition of some object of thought but an awareness in which the whole man is engaged (involving and causing, normally, some sensation). It is a body-soul reaction to a mystical reality, namely, the divine encounter with man. It has nothing to do with emotional feelings except insofar as the spiritual reaction of mind and will has some subsequent effect on the emotions.

The point is made succinctly by Jacques Maritain:

The phrase mystical experience I take . . . not in the more or less vague sense (applicable to all kinds of facts more or less mysterious or preternatural or even to simple religiosity) but in the sense of an experimental knowledge of the depths of God, or of the suffering of divine things, leading the soul, by a series of states and transformations to the point of realizing in the depths of self the touch of the deity.*

Sacred History is the history of religious experiences: God intervening in human affairs, revealing Himself, inviting and readying man to reach the pinnacle of all human experiences —the personal encounter with the living God. The cosmic and Mosaic revelation represents nothing more than a stage in mankind's advance in the knowledge of the true God. It is only in Jesus Christ that the hidden God is truly revealed: "No man has seen God at any time: the only-begotten Son who is in the bosom of the Father, he has declared him." God has expressed His fullness in the Word.

The Incarnation is the high point of religious experience: the divine-human encounter. And the Church is the prolongation of the Incarnation. The code and cult of the Church are meaningless apart from religious experience. They are either conceptual interpretations of religious experience (doctrine)

* *The Degrees of Knowledge* (New York: Chas. Scribner's Sons). This is actually a paraphrase of Maritain's statements on p. 247.

or the external, physical, cultural embodiments of religious experience (liturgy). Whatever is unrelated to this spiritual center is ecclesiastical materialism. In the light of this it seems that what is defective about our religious revival today is that most of us are spending all of our time and energy running around the circumference, and taking for granted the center which is religious experience.

We have shied away from the term "religious experience" ever since the Protestant revolution with its false and disastrous forms of "experiencing." Shall we discard religious experience because we have read or heard about neuropathic perversions or concomitants of religious experience? Do we condemn sex because we know of morbidities, hysteria, and perversions which abound in the sexual sphere? We think it is unreasonable to reject religious experience as subjective illusion, when in power, satisfaction, and delight, and in its value, intellectual and spiritual, it incalculably exceeds any other form of human experience.

What, then, is mystical theology? It is the theology of the fullness of the Christian life lived in union with Christ and the total Christ, the Church, and lived in such a way that it is experienced as well as understood. Mystical theology is bound up with what has been called by the Apostles and early Fathers "the mystery"—the living mystery of Christ on earth being born, living, redeeming the times, and dying day by day and rising again in the life of Christians. "No longer I but Christ lives in me."

Any deep spiritual life is a mystical life. If we define mystical life as that in which the direct action of God through the gifts of the Holy Spirit is predominant, we cannot conceive the possibility of living the spiritual life in any other way.

Extraordinary favors and thrilling experiences are not part of the mystical life. The life of St. Thomas, and even the lives of Mary and Joseph, is the living illustration and affirmation that the highest mystical life may be (and often is) without any appearance of mystical phenomena.

Mysticism is the passionate longing of the soul for God, the Unseen Reality, loved, sought, and adored in Himself and for Himself alone. A mystic is not a person who engages in unusual forms of prayer, but a person whose life is ruled by this thirst. He feels and responds to the overwhelming attraction of God, is sensitive to that attraction. He need not be a great religious personality, but he must be a servant of the Word. In other words, he may not vibrate to the presence of Christ, but he can know and cleave to Him nevertheless.

When we get away from the pure, simple declarations of truth in the inspired account of Christ's life, so vital, so full of love and quiet joy; when we get away from the real lives of the saints, so thoroughly human, we tend to create our own unreal idea of sanctity, our own imaginary brand of saint.

Look at us, with our refined, precise program of spirituality and our scientific studies of religion, our accumulated experience of centuries, our advanced education, our psychological discoveries; all this plus spiritual books, retreats, meditations, and liturgical exercises—and still, with all this machinery at our disposal and plentiful evidence of good will, we do not find many really great, convincing Christians among us. Not many saints. Why not? I venture to say it is due, principally, to one simple cause: we are afraid to live fully. We are not human enough. No, right from the outset, from an utterly false notion of piety, we dare not let ourselves become human beings. A human being is made, not born.

When we become perfectly human, we are saints. But we do not become perfectly human by our own power alone. Christ came to divinize us, make us like God, enrich us with divine life, life that would never diminish or grow dull with age or boredom. The Church, the contemporary Christ, has the same purpose; so has grace, the gift of divine life, supervitality. It is a mistake to think the only purpose of grace is to help us keep the commandments, to make us better, improved men, with nicer manners. To think this way is to miss the whole point of what our Lord means by being reborn, of all that St. Paul has to say about "newness of life," being "alive to God," and "all aglow with the Spirit." The purpose of grace is to make us richly, exuberantly alive.

We must not forget that grace needs a deep, reliable, healthy, natural ground if it is to take root and bear fruitfully; that otherwise the supernatural remains in the air, is unnatural, a phantom without strength or lifeblood.

And so there's got to be a basic hunger and thirst, a spontaneous zest for life. Have you ever noticed whom it is our Lord takes special pains to commend? The pagan centurion, the woman of the streets. Who is the only man in the world to whom God ever promised heaven? A thief. And the heroes of His favorite parables are the prodigal son and the good Samaritan. It is the Scribes and Pharisees, with their strict but heartless fidelity to the Law, whom He denounces. He calls them "whited sepulchres." Exactly: they were closed and opposed to lighthearted joy and mirth, to love, freedom, and good fellowship that ought to (indeed, must!) characterize the children of God.

In this context Bernanos' question makes impressive good sense: "Won't damnation be the tardy discovery, the discovery much too late, after death, of a soul absolutely unused, still carefully folded together, and spoiled, the way precious silks are spoiled when not used?"

And so the saint is one who lives life to the hilt. We are not saints because we are afraid of our own weaknesses and of the difficulties of life. Instead of giving ourselves enthusiastically to life, we approach it halfheartedly. By impoverishing the life of the spirit, we heighten the temptation of the world, the flesh, and the devil. As St. Thomas says: "No man can live without delight, and that is why a man deprived of spiritual joy goes over to carnal pleasures."

We don't begin to live once we've solved our problems. We solve our problems by living. That's what our Lord meant when He spoke of losing your life in order to save it: in other words, don't try to save it by guarding and hoarding it carefully, fretfully, but by living it, spending it rightfully, bravely, unstintingly.

But if the Christian life is so vital, so positive, and affirmative, then what's all this insistence on self-denial, mortification, detachment?

A full life and great love: this is the dutiful goal of every Christian.

Clearly we are here faced with paradox. We are to love

and yet to hate; the earth is dark and tempting yet it is God's earth, God's gift to us, and ceaselessly it gives Him glory; we are to be mortified and treat earthly things as of no account, yet we are to love the lilies of the field, to reverence the hallowed mystery of human love, to delight in the wine that "rejoiceth the heart of man"; what is the answer to the paradox?

It is based on a very sound principle: two contraries cannot exist in the same subject at the same time. For instance, communism and capitalism cannot coexist in America. I cannot move north and south at the same time. I cannot serve two masters. My affections cannot be absorbed by creatures and by God.

The word "detachment" has a negative ring to it, and for this reason it does not seem unwise for us to prefer to term it "poverty of spirit." It seems easier to see "poverty" as positive: unattached but full of concern and deeply in love. Not that it is necessary or even desirable to rule out negation for the sake of accentuating the positive. It isn't even possible. We must not cater to an unrealistic, unbalanced humanism—acting as if grace were an injection that by itself turned our natural lives into a most pleasing service of God without our constant, heroic effort to live full lives of Christian virtue.

No one can become full unless there's an emptiness to be filled. No one can receive a gift unless he has space to receive it, unless he is receptive. Supernatural life is a gift from God. The way to receive it is to become empty, open, receptive, making room for God's onrush.

So the first step toward fullness, the first aspect of detachment, is emptiness. Not a meaningless, gaping void, but a constructive emptiness, like the hollow in a reed—a space to receive and form the piper's breath and to express the song in his heart; like the emptiness of a chalice, above all, like the purposeful emptiness of our Lady's virginity. There was nothing more positive than our Lady's emptiness. In her emptiness God became man.

It takes courage and trust to empty oneself and wait for the advent of Christ. But it is worth it. Do you remember the story of the Dutch boy who by putting his finger into the hole in the dike prevented the water from flooding Holland? Well, that unfortunately is what we do when we spoil our emptiness by allowing even one single attachment to one creature prevent the ocean of God's love from flooding our souls.

Even after Christ has come there will be denials, negations, mortifications. It figures. What happens when a boy meets a girl who catches his eye and his heart? He makes sacrifices. A sacrifice is a living expression of a preference. The boy denies himself the time he used to spend so fondly with boys at the club because he prefers to be with her, denies himself certain luxuries and pleasures because he prefers to spend his money for her. Well, that's what happens when you get to know Christ and begin really to love Him. It is inevitable.

It is important to see this real meaning of sacrifice in order to avoid the fatal misunderstandings in our popular versions of sanctity.

Self-denial leads to self-mastery, yes. We lost self-mastery, integrity, with the fall of our first parents. Integrity was not returned to us by Christ's Redemption. We received instead a really better gift: the gift of actual graces "tailored" to suit each moment of our lives and each need of our personalities. By the aid of these graces and our own effort we are meant to restore balance and harmony to our humanity. We gain mastery not by renouncing human nature, but by renouncing anarchy. Becoming deliberately human is extremely difficult; nothing is more easily or more often shirked. Renouncing the inhuman or subhuman in one's life is more painful than a lifetime of hairshirts and fasting.

But there is a more valuable point to sacrifice than that. Sacrifice is giving—giving something to God; something fine, precious, given with joy and liberality.

We sometimes speak and act as if it were the pain and loss sustained in giving that are the most important features; as if it were self-inflicted misery that God takes pleasure in. This is dreadfully wrong. We don't give in order to hurt ourselves; we give to please the receiver. The pain accompanying the gift is at most the price of our precious right to give, and we do not haggle or complain about it—nor are we proud of it.

There is another cogent reason for mortification compatible with stressing of the positive and affirming of good found in creatures. All spiritual emotions and high resolves die unless nourished. We are sometimes surprised and chagrined at our own loss of zeal and piety and at the inability to pray as we once did. One day, like the startled bridesmaids of the Gospel, we wake up and see smoking wicks instead of brilliant flames. The snuffed flame is a result of our doing nothing; luxuriating in a status quo, just sleeping, like the bridesmaids. Most lives are not ruined through wickedness, but through the gradual gathering of grease and scum when not stirred by sacrifice.

And so we can understand why, along with the bright, vivid life theme of the Gospels, there is a strong undercurrent theme of death. Rebirth implies death. Grass must die in order to enjoy the higher life of a cow; a cow must undergo death before she can take part in the higher life of man; and a man dies to himself in order to live in Christ.

Even our Lord followed this principle of loss and gain. The purpose of Calvary was not the death of Christ but the resurrection; and the purpose of renunciation is not to annihilate life but to increase it, to further the life of grace and the life of nature as well. The rightness of renunciation must be judged by the intensity of life that results from it, by the openhearted attitude of acceptance that results from it. The tendency to renounce and restrict one's vitality is, as a rule, something that must be kept subservient to the more important, positive effort of accepting.

The first achievement of life is the main thing, but that life comes only through some kind of death. Life, the development of all vital potentialities, obviously requires great effort even if lived on a purely natural level. Life means choice and renunciation. To choose what is human, to live at all worthily, is to renounce what is inhuman. The life without choice is not worth living.

The sacrifice of all is eagerly made by one desiring to

possess the one thing beside which all else is worthless. Such singleheartedness involves renunciation but not refusal of life, not timidity in living. To count the whole world well lost for a cause or a person is to live with sincerity and vivid directness. When, therefore, a man comes alive to God, he responds with alacrity to his challenge: "If thou wilt be perfect, go sell what thou hast and give to the poor—and thou shalt have treasure in the heavens—and come follow me."

And so, like the saints, we must not be afraid to live; and our mortifications will be chosen in view of greater life until we come magnificently alive with supernatural life.

Neither must we be afraid to love. Detachment does not mean that we love nothing but God; it means, rather, that we love everything in God; it does not mean we learn to love creatures less and less; it means, rather, that we learn to love creatures more and more; but it means loving them in God, not apart from God.

In our efforts to become detached we must never destroy our love for anyone or anything. The only thing we are permitted to kill is the one thing that spoils our love: selfishness. This is the function of mortification—to kill all forms of selfishness, thus liberating the person from enslavement to any creature and empowering him with an intense and universal love. It is no longer a limited, imperfect, sin-ridden, possessive love, but the healing, saving love of Christ.

How do we detect selfishness? When we find we are using God's creatures not for His honor and glory but for our own, seizing upon things or people for our own pride, profit, and pleasure. When we find we are reaching and grabbing instead of standing with reverence before the sacredness of things, then there is selfishness. When we allow a creature to compete with God for the possession of our hearts, when our love is divided between God and someone else, then there is selfishness.

How do we kill the multiheaded dragon of selfishness and put order into our love? By mortification; not a wholesale program of mortification; but just that kind of mortification (no more dates with Jim, or no more phone calls to Sue, or no TV for a while, or more kindness to that unpleasant neighbor, or much more courtesy or concentrated study) that will remedy this kind of disordered love, and for as long a time as it will take to bring order out of chaos. Suppose, for instance, if you are a young person, that the time you spend with the gang prevents study and prayer and sufficient rest; then that's the thing to mortify; cut your time spent with the gang down to a minimum. Suppose your business consumes so much of your time that you have no time left for your family or for a decent, leisurely celebration of Sunday; then that's the thing to mortify. If you find that your most frequent distraction in prayer is the tendency to daydream; then that's the thing to mortify.

We cannot use created things for the glory of God unless we are in control of ourselves. We cannot be in control of ourselves if we are under the power of the desires and appetites and passions of the flesh. We cannot give ourselves to God if we do not belong to ourselves. And we do not belong to ourselves if we belong to creatures.

The real function of renunciation is, then, to liberate us from desires that debase and enslave us to creatures. The real purpose of self-denial is to turn over the faculties of our soul and body to the Holy Spirit in order that He may work in us the work of transformation which is His masterpiece.

A detached person, is, therefore, a perfectly pure and transparent instrument of Christ. Through him Christ lives on in our world praising His Father, saving men, redeeming the world. This is so true that God is able to look down on such a detached person and say: "This is My beloved Son in Whom I am well pleased."

The detached person himself, like St. John of the Cross, will be able to say: "Mine are the hills and the mountains are mine, mine are the just and the sinners are mine, the nations are mine, the people are mine, the Mother of God is mine, God Himself is mine and for me, because Christ is mine and all for me."

We are not born human. We are born with the primitive, shapeless stuff of humanity. It takes colossal and consistent effort to become really human. It demands, most of all divine favor; and for that we need a mediator.

Adam and Eve walked with God. And they talked with Him. It involved no great effort at all. It was just the spontaneous response of our unsullied first parents as they strolled leisurely through Eden's lush pastures in God's company. They were electrically aware of God's presence. All their human activity was centered and focused on Him. Wanting nothing for their perfection, desiring nothing outside of God for their happiness, they were filled to the brim; and they enjoyed God.

Adam, the first man, called to share by grace in the divine life, represented in God's eyes the whole of mankind. Adam's fall was the fall of mankind. Separated from God, the only source and goal of life, mankind, like some dizzy planet detached from its sun, revolved in aimless convolutions around itself. Man dethroned God and enthroned himself. And his throne throttled his deeper human aspirations, threatened his life and fettered him to the earth. His own self became the center of his striving and yearning. Man came to feel God, the source of his life, as a burden. But man cannot live without God. So man fell sick and died. Selfishness made him sick; it was his primal sin; it was his death. And all mankind —incurably self-centered—died with him. So with supernatural life gone, flung away by Adam for himself and all his descendants by the common law of inheritance, men and women were born into the world with no natural hope of ever again living a Godlike life. Men and women were born dead; and criminals too.

Between God and man there was no longer any relationship except that of dependence heightened and deepened and stained deep crimson by a horrible crime that all of human tears could not wash away. Man had deliberately broken the bonds of love and friendship between himself and God. There remained only the relationship of a rebellion for which man could make no reparation.

His crime was against an infinite God. His repentance must continue to be always the apology of a finite being. The crime was direct from man to God. The repentance could only be the puny act of one small rebel who, to wage war against Him had used all the blessings and favors and the very existence given him by his Maker.

Having rebelled against God, man was deprived of his right to his adopted sonship, excluded from his inheritance of eternal happiness, supernaturally dead and incapable of seeing, knowing, loving, and possessing God, a criminal guilty of a crime beyond the reach of any apology he can offer or any reparation he can make.

The Old Testament is the story of how God reeducated mankind, readying it, bit by bit, to receive the divine gifts He destined for it. The whole purpose of the Old Testament was to prepare for Him who was to come. The sacred history of the centuries between Adam's fall and Christ's coming is a record of the *mirabilia Dei* (the wonderful works of God).

And so God made a natural covenant with Noah, and He chose Abraham, gracing and favoring His race in view of things to come. He sent His angels like messengers of lightning to break down the barriers between man and God. He raised up prophets, spiritual giants of humanity with a wonderful awesome sense of God, with keen insight into His divine plan, and a remarkable talent for defending the rights of God with vehemence, and denouncing the egregious folly of man with acrimonious invective. They were powerful men, but they were finite men. Their achievements, therefore, were always limited, and sometimes nullified. But they did what they could, expending themselves unremittingly for God's purposes; but in the end they pointed to Him who was to come.

And He came. "Sacrifice and oblation thou wouldst not; then said I: 'Behold, I come.'"

At that point the most singular event in the history of the

world unfolded. It marked the pinnacle of all human achievements. It was the epitome of all that went before, the ineluctable center of all that would follow. For at that moment a Man was born who in the first split second that He was conceived recognized who He was and why He existed. A human soul, a mind with infinite range, a will capable of limitless love, which a moment before did not exist, began to exist and saw immediately with shimmering clarity and unlimited comprehension, without being dazzled or frightened—saw who He was.

He saw who He was because when He came alive He was looking with all of His might and all of His heart into the face of God whom He recognized at once as His Father. And this Man was able to say with infallible certainty and divine serenity: "I am God."

That was the human experience of Christ at the moment of His birth. "I am God" means so many things. And Christ expressed it in various ways: I am the Vine, you are the branches; I am the Way, the Truth, and the Life; all power is Mine in heaven and on earth; all things are delivered to Me, and no one knows the Son but the Father: neither does anyone know the Father but the Son, and he to whom it shall please the Son to reveal Him. I am the Door. By Me, if any man enter in he shall be saved; without Me you can do nothing.

"I am God" coming from man could mean only one thing: the unbridgeable gap between God and man was bridged. The transcendent, inaccessible, devouring God of might and majesty was not only close to man, abiding with him; He *was* Man. The Word was made flesh. God became Man. The result of this unique and stupendous historical incident was that the human race now had one Man who was really what all men were meant to be: one Man in whom there was absolutely nothing to impede or trammel His total and immediate and irrevocable response to God. The natural and the human creature in Him were taken up fully into the divine Son. Thus, in one instance humanity had, so to speak, arrived: had passed into the life of Christ.

Because Christ is the everlasting Man, this divine-human

condition of humanity lasts forever. And because He is the Head of humanity, what He was and what He did affects the life of every man. You can put it this way: just as the fall of Adam from God's grace and favor left all of his descendants a way of life that was darkened and hampered and crippled at every turn; so the rise of Christ as the new Head of humanity has a healing and ennobling and transforming effect on the life of every man. God, who did not cease to govern and sustain the human race because of Adam, begins to enliven the whole human mass in a new and unspeakably wonderful way because of Christ. Not only because of Him, but through and in Him. From that incarnational point the effect spreads through all mankind. It makes a difference to people who lived before Christ, as well as to people who lived after Him. It makes a difference to people who have not even heard of Him and who, perhaps, never will. When God became Man there was revolution, reform, and renewal at the core of the human world. It's like dropping one tiny particle of saccharine into a cup of coffee, giving the whole drink a new taste.

No wonder we started counting the years all over again. Christ started something new—a new heaven and a new earth: a new heaven because where God is, there is heaven; and a new earth because of the radical change in man who rules and subdues the earth. The Incarnation did not necessarily mean that there would be better, improved men, with nicer manners. It meant a whole world of brand new men, transformed, elevated to a new level of nature. It is an indescribably deep change—from being creatures of God to being sons of God.

The chief purpose of the Incarnation was to begin on earth the kind of life God lives eternally in heaven. This happened when God became Man, and the canticle of love which the Word sang from all eternity in the bosom of God now emanated with the same richness and worth from the human heart of Christ, who marches before the generations of men with a song of love and praise in His heart, and a single word on His lips, namely: Eternally Father.

And so there was one Man in the world in whom the

created life, derived from His Mother, was completely and perfectly attuned to the divine life begotten of God. There was one God-centered Man. There was one Man magnificently and gloriously alive with the Trinitarian life of God.

The mystery of the Incarnation has three-dimensional ramifications that have not even begun to be exhausted by all the theology ever written. But just as "all things were recapitulated and summed up in Christ," so can this infinite variety of deep-seated, world-wide consequences be summed up, or at least suggested by a phrase that came like a triumphant thunderclap from the blazing spirit of St. Paul: "We have a Pontiff . . . Jesus Christ, Son of God." These few words make up a very small and simple declarative sentence. But it is a sentence that is packed with more meaning, power, and glory than any other ever recorded in human archives. And it resounds in the bosom of the Godhead. It expresses human aspiration and fulfillment that lie beyond the wildest human dream; it hints at the supreme and reckless ingenuity of divine love; it involves the throbbing, voiceless, exultant glory of the earth; it proclaims a truce to all figures and types, prophecies, images, and shadows, and announces the permanent, enduring reality of Christ, the great High Priest who in His own Person summarizes the multiform victims that had been offered to God and draws together in their fullness the priesthoods, from that of Abel, sacrificing at his primitive altar, through Melchisedech, offering bread and wine, to the high priests of the Mosaic sacrifices. "For there is one God and one Mediator of God and men, the Man, Jesus Christ."

In all of the grand sources of theology—Scripture, Tradition, the Fathers, and in St. Thomas as well—you can find no better word to express the nature and mission of Christ than "priest."

Almost the whole Epistle to the Hebrews is an amplification of St. Paul's realization that Christ is "called by God a High Priest according to the order of Melchisedech. . . . For it was fitting that we should have a high priest, holy, innocent, undefiled, separated from sinners; and made higher than the heavens; who needed not daily (as the other priests) to offer sacrifices first for his own sins, and then for the people's; for this he did once in offering himself."

There is only one priesthood—that of Christ. Others have had some participation of the priesthood; He has it in its entirety, or rather it is not so much that He has it as that He *is* it. He is the whole priesthood. So He is not a Priest among priests, more powerful and holy than they. He is the Unique Priest. He includes all priesthood in Himself.

Christ has not merely fulfilled the function of a priest, He was a Priest; and He was so from the first moment of His mortal life, intrinsically, and in all His acts. He was and is essentially a Priest in virtue of the Incarnation (the Hypostatic Union). This teaching has been luminously illustrated by all patristic and theological tradition. Both show that the priesthood of Christ is derived directly from His Incarnation. "The Word who is at once the perfect image of the Father and the exemplar of creation, from the time of the Incarnation cannot be other than the Mediator, the religious bond between God and man, and consequently the priest."

That is why the Savior could afford to lie in the straw, walk through the fields, work quietly in His father's shop, remain hidden most of His life: He was mediating just by being Himself, the God-Man. "God was in Christ reconciling the world to Himself."

Mediation, according to St. Thomas, is the essential note of priesthood. "The proper office of the priest is to be a mediator between God and the people, insofar as he transmits divine things to the people . . . and insofar as he offers the prayers of the people to God, and somehow satisfies for their sins. . . ." Mediation is, likewise, the key to the scriptural and traditional aspects of the Incarnation and Redemption which underlie Christ's priestly work of reconciliation. Christ is the perfect Mediator and the unique Mediator: (1) by His very constitution as God and Man, and (2) by His infinite work of redemption. Christ is man's only access to the Father. Apart from Him and His priestly work of mediation, there is no salvation. Take away either the completeness of His divinity or the completeness of His humanity and the picture is spoiled; for while He is Unique Priest and Mediator as

Man, this is true only because He is also God. The substantial mediation of the Incarnate Word is manifested to mankind by His life, words, and works of priestly mediation, especially by His sacrifice on Calvary. Since His priesthood and priestly mediation are eternal, they still exist for men today. Christ is the Living Bridge between God and man.

4 · A REAL CHRIST

Christ is not only our mediator. He is "God in His most attractive form," and ought to be, therefore, the most magnetic and influential force in our lives.

To date, the biggest hole in our educational system is the failure to convey to young students a meaningful, vital awareness of Christ. This conclusion is the result of years of experience, during which Catholic high school and college students and adults in all parts of the country were examined as to their impressions and knowledge of Christ, and as to the part He played in their lives. The general response was not good.

Their ideas were vague, general, unreal, sentimental, impersonal, academic. To many Christ was a myth, to others merely a historical figure; to others divine all right, but quite remote and not an influence in their everyday life. But a religion without Christ is a corpse; an education that does not convey ideas of Christ that are vital, real, precise, and compelling is a farce. If people are ready to worship a hero and follow a leader, then it is a mistake to obscure the person of Christ behind a welter of abstractions. If they are going to be raised to a higher stature, it will not be by moral coercion or intellectual persuasion, not even by the high ideal of becoming perfect, a saint.

Such an ideal is too abstract; and most people need something concrete, dynamic, highly personal to shape their thinking and influence their behavior. They need the infinitely attractive personality of Christ. Nothing else will catch and hold their attention, engage their interest, and fill their heart as Christ will. Christ lived a life so captivatingly lovable that it is enough to tear the heart out of anyone who will become acquainted with it. Who can help but be influenced by the irresistible force of Him who said: "And I, if I be lifted up, I will draw all things to myself"?

It is impossible to look into the face of Christ without being drawn into the action of Christ. That is what François Mauriac meant when he said: "Once you get to know Christ, you cannot be cured of Him." That is also why you will never see a crucifix in a Discalced Carmelite cell. Every Carmelite wears one on his heart, for there is none on the bare walls of the cell; just the empty cross. The reason for this is the difference between the crucifix and the cross. The crucifix is a memorial to a crucified God, but a cross is an invitation to a real Christian. It is the divine call and challenge to do what He did for the glory of His Father and the redemption of the world.

All must be taught, therefore, to believe not only in a creed but through a creed in a person. Faith must come to mean to them what it meant to St. Bonaventure: "a habit of the mind whereby we are drawn and captivated into the following of Christ." Religion will thus cease to be a moral code, a list of forbidding commandments, a dull, drab affair. It will take on the thrill and excitement of a love affair between God and man. It will mean, above all, a friendship with Christ.

There are two things, therefore, that all of us have to learn: how and where to read the life of Christ, and how to pray. This chapter does not develop these two points; it simply attempts to show why they must be developed.

What does He mean to you? Have you not been as long as you can remember groping for something that has eluded you, grasping at one thing and then another, captivated again and again by new vistas of life that opened up suddenly, unexpectedly, yet left you at the end, still wandering disillusioned, restless?

Like all the rest of us you wanted a companion. You could not bear to live alone; you wanted and needed someone with whom to share the adventure of life—the unpredictable joy of it, the inevitable pain of it. And so you attached yourself to another heart the same size as your own, but inevitable conditions of life deprived you of it. Then you went in search for another to lean on, love, and share joy and sorrow with. But there was something fleeting, futile, and unsatisfying about them all.

The secret of it all dawned on you one day. You had been looking the wrong way, searching far off when the soul-satisfying object of your hunger and your striving was within your grasp all the time. All the time you had a companion:

a baby in your babyhood, a child in your childhood, a youth beside your youth—happy when you were happy, sorrowing when you were sorrowful, as triumphant as yourself over your victory; no more than you and yet enclosing you, accepting all the love that you were capable of giving and giving so much more in return; hungering more than you hungered, and putting your hunger to shame; so that henceforth your tiny little hunger forgot its own hunger in its longing to satisfy this other hungry heart whose cravings mattered so much more.*

God loves you, He loves me, He loves us all. He became man to reveal this to us. He died to prove this to us. "Greater love than this no man has than to lay down his life for a friend." And for our sake He did not come down from the cross. His enemies teased Him to come down. It would have been a terrific moment full of glory and triumph. He could have proved so many things; He could have forced His enemies to eat their words; He could have consoled His Mother, reclaimed His scattered following, and vindicated Himself.

But He did not come down. Why not? Because you and I were not there. He wanted to walk not only over the hills of Palestine and on the waters of Genesareth; He wanted to walk on the hills of New England and the waters of America. He wanted to possess the hearts not only of Mary and Peter and John but all the hearts of all the people in the world for all time.

For this He had to die and come alive again in His Mystical Body with a life just as real and dynamic and revolutionary as was His physical life. "I have loved you unto the end. . . . I am with you all days, even to the consummation of the world." Such is the exigency of love. It is the nature of friends to spend their days delighting in one another. So

* Archbishop Goodier, unpublished.

spoke Aristotle, the philosopher. So lives Christ, the relentless Lover.

Have you ever really known what it means to love? Do you know what is love unsatisfied, endured in loneliness, ready to burst your restless, ravenous heart? Do you know what it is to have the intolerable strain suddenly removed, the void suddenly filled up, to have found Him whom your soul has always loved, to have held Him, and never to let Him go?

If not, you have not come to know Jesus Christ. He is the Pied Piper of human hearts. He turns human lives inside out like gloves. He transforms weak, hesitant fishermen into strong, ardent champions of God. He makes men walk on water and live as carefree as birds.

Christ is the invisible Piper piping through all the streets of the world. He is the Catholic Church in the world. Other religious, social, and political organizations may arouse opposition, but the incurable disquietude of those who fear the Catholic Church is due to the fact that while all others are systems, the Church is a Person, an incalculable Person, a Person with infinite power and a child's values, the Person of Jesus Christ.

There is no decent response to His attraction other than irrevocable commitment. Once a man follows Him he no longer desires to satisfy his own loves, but desires instead to satisfy with all his life the love of Another. He no longer seeks pleasure in love, but forgets his existence in a new ardent love. His own delight in love is to suffer and to live in order to give, to endure, to labor.

One day when F. D. Roosevelt was President he met a lad on the corner selling newspapers. He casually asked the little fellow what he planned to do with the money he made on the papers. The boy answered that he intended to build a city as large as New York. The President laughed. The boy went on to explain that it wasn't so funny or impossible after all because my "buddy is down on the next corner; and he is also selling papers; we are working on this thing together."

That was the foundation of his bold and daring project: working together and with a friend. It wasn't quite valid in his case because his friend was as human as he and could only contribute an extremely limited amount to the cause. But in our case, working together with our friend, Christ, Son of the living God, is a valid foundation for the most daring, superhuman endeavors. Like St. Paul, Joan of Arc, Theresa, and the other saints, we can do all things in Him who strengthens us, who buoys us up, who has already overcome the world.

It is a unique and unspeakably wonderful kind of friendship. Christ is like us and yet is infinitely perfect. He is so down to earth and yet God of heaven and earth. He takes delight in our company and yet all creation cannot contain Him. He knows us through and through—our shame, our sinfulness, our cowardice—and yet loves us with an everlasting love. He will never forsake us no matter how repulsive we may become to human company. He will never let us suffer alone, no matter how degraded and despicable our suffering may be. And He will never have a private sort of joy or sorrow because of us.

His love has transformed ours, not crushed it. Although we love no one besides Christ, we do love all in Christ. He has not taught us to love things less and less for the sake of His friendship; we have learned to love them with His eyes and love them with His heart. Now we know what love means; not the cramped, limping, narrowed, self-indulgent thing that so many fancy it to be, but the great, stouthearted, selfless, all-embracing thing that opens a man's heart to the dimensions of the universe, shaping it to the compass of Christ's own heart, giving man a certain kinship with God Himself.

Christ is the ideal Man. We will always be dissatisfied with even the loftiest specimens of mankind. No one of our noblest men is a spotless sun; no one reached sinless perfection—no one except Christ. In Him the ideal becomes actual, the dream real.

He is the fullest manifestation of divinity God has given to the world; He is the brightness of God's glory, and the very image of God's substance. He rises in unapproachable glory, not only above men, but also above saints and seraphs, above angels and archangels. Gazing upon Him we can exclaim with inexpressible enthusiasm and unutterable ecstasy, "He is Man!" and with the same breath and with equal truth we can also reverently exclaim, "He is God!"

We must not think of Christ as a dreamy, sentimental, and poetic character. Avoid nursery endearments. Christ is the great Exemplar, the perfect Model, the sublime Original to be imitated by all true men and women. In Him, and in Him only, the plant of humanity blossomed and blossomed into a perfect flower.

If you were to write down all the significant data about Christ, "the world," as St. John tells us, "would not contain the books that must be written."

It is easy to see that Christ possessed extraordinary physical charm: children loved Him, and those in any sort of trouble ran to Him. He was strong and virile: He rose early in the morning to pray and often spent whole nights in prayer; and very frequently He had nowhere to sleep but the open air. During his public life He always journeyed on foot, and with the minimum of provisions. Sometimes He stayed so long with the sick He took no time to eat.

He had an extraordinary knack of handling crowds. He had to be always on the alert, for His enemies were forever trying to catch Him up in a knot of irremediable error. Remember one incident? The scene is graphic, the lesson cogent. The Scribes and Pharisees are, as usual, plying Him with questions. Suddenly the tables are turned. Christ halts them, impales their quizzical, lusterless eyes on the fine point of His piercing, irresistible gaze; and He asks them questions.

This was an unforgettable instance among the Jews. Here was a carpenter's son, an uneducated man from Nazareth, questioning the doctors of the law, the elite, the intelligentsia. You could have hung your hat on the tension that shot out like a tangent from the regal commanding figure of Christ, to the encircling gloom of dumbfounded men.

The closest disciples are often a trial to Christ's patience because of their inability to understand and their narrowness of outlook. He had an insatiable thirst for life. It was to share this zest for life that He came into the world: "I come that you may have life and have it more abundantly."

He lived life eagerly. Only the strongest and healthiest physique could have borne the strain of so full a life. His last journey from Jericho to Jerusalem through rocky country and a blazing sun involved a climb of about 3500 feet in six hours; and it was at the end of this rugged haul—that would have exhausted the Fighting Irish of Notre Dame—that He took part in the banquet at Bethany with Lazarus and his sisters.

The exquisite sovereignty of His mind was obvious in every situation at every moment. With clarity and assurance He knew exactly what His mission was. Notice the number of times He says: I come for this or that purpose, I do not come for this other. Never any hesitation, doubt, or compromise. He was always direct, candid, genuine.

Some people are disturbed by the fact that Christ was, on rare occasions, stern and angry: they feel something incompatible between this harshness and the more characteristic gentleness of the Lord. But these qualities are part of the same fullness of the Son of God. If you love humanity, you must hate inhumanity; if you enjoy a perfect vision of truth, you will be that much more thoroughly set against deceit and falsehood. Christ was not just a romantic and sentimental humanitarian, in whom moral indignation and righteous anger would be out of place.

Christ was not an impossible sort of idealist. He loved us unto the end all right; but all the time He was aware of our selfishness, cowardice, and infidelity, the horrible fact of malice, hatred, and gross evil, and He gave us pity and mercy, and undying love just the same. Remember the publican, the adulteress, the Lord's gentleness with Judas, and His forgiveness of Peter.

Our Lord's delicate and precise concern for the little things of life is most precious. The roads and fields of Palestine were companion to His life and work. The poor were His delight, and sinners the object of His love and attention. Children seemed to be the specially favored creatures of His whole kingdom. He loved to toy reverently and significantly with trees, flowers, water, wind, sand, and stars. Nothing escapes His love and care.

Jesus is far more than a mere man, far more even than the greatest historical figure. He is God. You can admire and extol historical figures; but you don't fall in love with them. It is impossible to know Christ without falling in love with Him. It is important, therefore, to cultivate a sharp awareness of the divinity of Christ. "He that sees me sees the Father. . . . Behold a greater than Solomon is here. . . . I tell you there is here a greater than the temple. . . . The Son of Man is Lord of the Sabbath. . . . He that loveth father and mother more than me is not worthy of me. . . . I am the Bread of Life. . . . I am the Way, the Truth, and the Life. . . . Before Abraham was made, I am. . . . You shall see the Son of Man coming in clouds of glory. . . ."

Christ introduced a whole new era into the world—an era of love. He cured the deaf, the blind, the crippled; and He raised the dead to life—all on His own authority. Never in His life did He betray any hint of a personal sense of sin. His prayer, too, is unique; there is complete absence of awe, fear, and penitence; but just the highest pitch of intimate, loving communion—unbroken by spiritual crises and upheavals that you find in other great men of prayer.

No law of heredity can account for the physical attractiveness, the mental superiority, and the moral perfection of Jesus. Neither can environment, nor education. Yet even His enemies were constrained to say: "No man ever spoke like this man." Who else could utter anything akin to the Sermon on the Mount? The foremost thinkers of today barely understand the social and religious significance of the Beatitudes. In pure spirituality of thought it is surpassed only by our Lord's last discourse to His disciples. This farewell address bears the ineffaceable marks of His divinity.

Remember that terrific scene when the Lord is walking triumphantly into Jerusalem and the people are spreading palms before Him and shouting alleluias of praise? Well, as you recall, the big men, the Scribes and Pharisees—envious of this adulation—protested and commanded Christ to forbid such demonstrations of loyalty and affection. And it was then that Christ said: "If they should be silent, the very stones would cry out."

No wonder He had such amazing, instantaneous effect upon the disciples. He said to them "Come after me . . ." and immediately leaving their nets they followed Him. It is as complete and absolute a commitment as that. He is like a potter with his clay.

Do you realize what a tremendous thing it was that He should emancipate Himself from the sectarianism and the sectionalism of His country and century, and become the contemporary of all ages?

This man—without outer trappings or forces, alone, single-handedly, by His inherent virtue and strength—lifted with His pierced hands empires off their hinges, and turned the stream of centuries out of its channel, introduced a brand new era with brand new men (not merely better ones), and still governs the ages.

Now, this Christ is the God who dwells within us; who is closer to us than we are to ourselves; who is more real than we are. We are real to the extent that we are in touch with His reality; we are alive to the degree that we respond to His activity.

What is His activity? Making friends out of human stuff. He is always at it—loving, hounding, wooing, enticing—until there is an adequate response from the human person, which means complete capitulation before the devastating demands of a jealous Lover, absolute surrender to the relentless chase of the divine Friend.

How does our response shape up? The first element is knowledge—a progressive enlightenment of the mind through spiritual reading (especially the life of Christ, more especially the New Testament), intelligent discussion, mental prayer (daily), and the consistent effort to live in the presence of God.

The second is love, a gradual enlargement of the heart through desiring, above all things and through all things, the friendship of Christ, through acts of love all day long (accepting everything from God, offering all to God, and sacrificing some things for God), through prayer (liturgical and private), and love of neighbor (not merely by avoiding evil but by a positive, tender care and solicitude).

The third element is commitment to Christ: Is our idea of Christ the biggest thing in our minds, or is it smothered and nullified by other ideas we get from movies, magazines, TV, cheap books, and idle chatter? Does He fill our souls like a riot of joy and sit on the edge of our lips like a shout of praise?

From now on we must have one single reason for everything we do; and that reason must be Christ.

What I am going to accentuate here and what I think needs to be accentuated in our Church, in our day, more than anything else is the personal structure of faith. This emphasis of the personal aspect of faith is meant in no way to minimize ecclesiastical faith, the organizational structure of the Church, the importance of dogma.

Faith leans on the word of God transmitted by the Holy Church. The Apostles transmitted the word of God with absolute authority and fidelity. This function is continued by the hierarchy until the end of time.

There is no faith except by the acceptance of the word of God; but the acceptance is only realized in full—on the level of intellect, love, and life—in the word of the Church of God.

Thus, to have faith is to believe not only a distant and purely invisible power of resurrection and life in Christ, but also in this power close at hand, expressed in the sacramental rite through which Christ takes hold of us, and rescuing us from our false self, makes us members of His body.

Even the faith by which people outside the Church are saved is the faith of the Church.

Now having said that without doubt or reservation, I will turn to the really great need of our day—the need for a *personal* faith in a real, live, personal God.

God speaks; man responds. But man is not forced to respond. He can respond to the world instead; as if it were the only reality, as if it were his supreme value. He can respond to himself; as if his own ego were the central, focal frame of reference, the sun which lights up and gives value to every other thing in his life. And yet a man is human, real, alive, only to the extent that he responds first and foremost, above and through all other things to God who speaks to him personally, calls him by name, loves him, and by His love creates and sustains him in being, and leads him unerringly to human fulfillment, divine union, vision, beatitude.

How can fallen man respond to the infinitely perfect love of
God, the devastating demands of God? There is only one
being who can respond adequately to God the Father's love
—and that is the Word, the Second Person of the Blessed
Trinity, who from all eternity sings His canticle of love in
the bosom of the Godhead.

But the Word was made flesh. All right then: here is the
single instance in the history of humanity when one man was
caught up fully into the divine life—one Man in whom there
was absolutely nothing to impede or trammel His total, immediate, and irrevocable response to God. What was natural,
human, created in Him was taken up fully into the divine
Son. Thus, in one instance humanity had, so to speak, arrived
—had passed into the life of Christ.

But the life of this one Man, this God-Man, has been prolonged and extended. This is mysteriously and wondrously
achieved by His Mystical Body. So if we want to respond to
God the Father who loves us, the first thing we have to do
is get into the Mystical Body, into Christ, share His divine
life, and utter His Word—the perfect response.

The "getting-in" bit is done, as St. Thomas Aquinas says,
by faith and the sacraments. And then the whole divinizing
process (transformation into Christ, putting on His mind,
coming to think like Him, love like Him, and act like Him)
which must follow is the development of faith.

That is why Scripture says that we cannot even begin to
approach God except by faith; we are children of God by
faith; the just man lives by faith.

And that is why our Lord insisted above all other things
on faith, on knowing Him. The crime of the Jews was not so
much that they did not love Him as that they did not know
Him. "He came unto his own and they did not know him."
He wept over Jerusalem because "they did not know the
things that pertained to their peace." Jesus refused to work
miracles in His favorite town "because there was no faith
there." The one question Christ wanted answered was the
one He asked at Caesarea Philippi: "What think ye of
Christ?" And toward the end of His life He said: "I no longer

call you servants but friends." Why? Because whatever He
has heard His Father say in the secrecy of the Godhead He
has shared with His followers. This is what it means to live
by faith: to be clued in by Christ, to be led right into the
heart of Trinitarian life—the family life of God—and share the
Son's secret knowledge of the Father. "And this is eternal life:
that you may know God and Jesus Christ whom he has sent."

The act of faith, according to St. Thomas, "is an act of the
intellect assenting to the divine truth at the command of the
will by the grace of God." While grace is a formal participation—created but real—in the divine nature, faith is a participation in the divine life considered as divine knowledge. It
is, says St. Thomas, "a light divinely infused in the mind of
man, a certain imprint of the First Truth." It is a constant
aptitude to know God as He knows Himself, to receive—according to the limited measure of created grace, it is true—
but really to receive the light from the dazzling Sun that is
God Himself. It is the sight of the supernatural life.

The act of the virtue of faith is, above all, a supernatural
act that goes far beyond the ordinary and limited field of
the activity of the intellect; it reaches out to God Himself,
to whom it adheres and makes the intellect and the whole
being of man adhere in an attitude of self-oblivious, adoring
assent. By an act of faith, the soul is borne into "a direct
exchange, an intimate union with the interior word of God.
. . . And as that interior Word not only existed at the time
of the manifestation of the exterior Word, but subsists, in
that it is the eternal word of God, in an eternal present, it
lifts up our mind to a participation in His supernatural truth
and life and makes it rest there."* This contact with the Deity Itself gives to the human person, in the words of St. Paul,
"the substance of things to be hoped for, the evidence of
things that are not seen" (Heb 2:1). It makes things real.
It makes us real; keeping us, as it does, in touch with ultimate reality, enabling us to view things as they really are,
giving us a veritable "possession of God, obscurely."

The act of faith is that which makes us adhere to the inner

* Scheeben, *Dogmatik*, I, 40, n. 681.

truth of revelation, to the divine reality itself revealed in human language.

St. John of the Cross is so emphatic about faith giving us God Himself. Beneath "the silvered surfaces" of the articles of faith, he says, there is the "gold of its substance." By this means alone, faith, God reveals Himself.

We must be careful not to develop a false faith—the kind that is easily preached and learned; the kind that kills liberty, initiative, and creativity. True faith enlists the vital forces of the human spirit in a judgment of values, a revitalization of self, and a proof of liberty. Faith does not adhere blindly to any formula. It opens itself to a presence. The complex system of dogmas, precepts, and rules that man imposes upon himself is meant to be used for the sake of transcendence and self-forgetful adoration. If a man lacks the courage or the intelligence to do this, if he refuses to transcend the system and the symbol, he is reciting formulas and making gestures, but he remains at the level of superstition and never reaches the higher, nobler plane of religion.

If he slothfully and smugly accepts the creed with no intelligent, personal re-creation of it in terms of his own unique and existential self, it is doubtful if he has faith at all; certainly not enough by which to live.

The man of faith does not sacrifice his freedom. He enters into faith through a system; he espouses the system and becomes part of it. But as soon as his faith becomes functional, that is, as soon as he prays and communicates with God, the system no longer dominates him; in fact, it is he who enlivens the system by opening himself to grace. His religious experience, intimate and incommunicable, though dependent on communal norms, is conceptualized in doctrine and embodied in ritual. The whole mechanism of rules and obligations is only a means, though an indispensable one. But once its end has been attained the person is set free; he is ruled and governed by love alone. It was to such a faithful, liberated man that St. Augustine said: "Love God and do what you will." St. John of the Cross, too, has plenty to say about this state of soul. But the pragmatists, the authoritarians, and the timid are very nervous about this sort of thing. They are wary of escapades outside the network of rules. To transcend the instruments of mediation seems to them to be a breach of religious loyalty. The opposite is true: we respect an instrument insofar as we use it properly; not idolize it.

It is possible for us to impede and restrain man's worship of God in faith if we become more devoted to the system than to what it represents or seeks to achieve. We must not loiter with an abstraction when we are after an essential value. We must not be unduly concerned with a theology of the things of God when we are bound to be concerned with the theology of God.

Now we can understand how faith cannot be an object of propaganda, of inheritance, or of personal possession. It does not spring forth made to order, nor is it born through imitation, nor will it endure merely through habit.

We must be very careful, too, about depersonalizing the whole concept of faith. Sometimes we try to be so neat and tidy in our explanation of faith that we smother its essentially personal element with abstractions. This has been done often enough, and the results have been disastrous.

Theology teaches that the primary object of faith is God in His Deity, in His own nature, in His intimate life, as He is in Himself. According to St. John of the Cross, we believe by faith the very object that God sees, and which we ourselves will see in heavenly beatitude.

St. Bonaventure's definition of faith saves us from the abstract: "it is the habit of mind whereby we are drawn and captivated into the following of Christ." We do not only believe in a creed; we believe through a creed in a Person. The ultimate object of our faith is always a personal encounter with a living God. This will always involve a unique kind of adventure and exploration. The articles of faith, therefore, are not meant to arrest our vision but to direct it. Dogmas are merely the intellectual means required for this final act of communion; and this communion is effected in secret between human freedom and the freedom of God.

Faith, though rooted in the intellect and oriented toward knowledge of God, is a response of the whole man; not just an activity of his isolated intellect. In fact, the most intimate,

experiential knowledge of God is more an effect of love than
of reasoning—this is mystical knowledge or contemplation: "a
pure intuition of God born of love" (Salmanticenses). Remember how the disciples on the way to Emmaus recognized
the risen Lord?—not by reason but by an act of love: "in the
breaking of bread."

Faith is not only an act; it is an attitude. It's the way we
look at the world: seeing everything against the background
of eternity; seeing the will of God unfolding in mysterious
ways; seeing the brilliant countenance of Christ or the Man
of Sorrows looking up at us from every creature; seeing oneself cradled and enveloped in God's personal love. It's a long
view, diametrically opposed to notions that are petty, narrow, shortsighted. It's a divine sort of sense of humor that
sees through people, things, events, and situations into the
plan of God.

If, therefore, a man lives by faith, he becomes rooted in
God. Then, no matter how seething and turbulent the surface
of life, he remains undisturbed, firmly fixed, as he is, in ultimate reality.

Faith is not only an act and an attitude; it is a commitment—an irrevocable commitment to Christ who said with
such irresistible magnetism, "if I be lifted up I will draw all
things to myself." Since then men of faith have been drawn
by the infinitely attractive personality of Christ. He is the
Pied Piper of human hearts—old and young. Christ makes
people become like little children and suddenly turns the
world in which they live upside down because they have
been enchanted and overwhelmed by Him.

Just because a man is committed to God by faith he should
not take himself too seriously. In fact, he ought to take God
so seriously that he regards himself quite lightheartedly. He
must make as little fuss as possible, bearing with himself and
others patiently, good-humoredly. He must remember that
regardless of his faith he is still a child of Adam.

Commitment implies renouncement. To live by faith is to
live for Christ; and it is harder to live for Christ than to die
for Him. Living one's faith to the hilt involves a daily death
(to all forms of selfishness). One can actually revel, take great

delight at the thought of being hanged, drawn, and quartered. But if God makes no revelation, no spectacular demands, but just goes on letting a man fulfill his life of faith in an ordinary, unpretentious, routine sort of way—that will require a greater kind of heroic commitment than being persecuted.

Faith is not static but dynamic. It must grow or it must stagnate. The man of stagnant faith is a religious moron. A man is as alive as his faith is. Even our Lady had to grow in faith.

Growth in faith, which is the "only proximate and immediate means of union with God," involves the necessary pain of being weaned away from purely human and sensible ways of knowing and loving Him—imagining, reasoning, feeling.

To grow in faith means, from the standpoint of the senses, that a man must welcome darkness, since he consecrated his life to a reality which he cannot see or feel, while he is constantly solicited by the call of his senses and of his passions, by the enticing mirage of the glittering beauty of the world of the senses.

To grow in faith means to live progressively in the spirit —by the intelligence and the will; and one cannot hope to do this except by mortifying the senses. Even the spirit's human mode of activity (intellectual concepts and purely human aspirations) cannot unite a man to God who is infinitely above and beyond all human modes of knowing and loving.

And so there will come a time in every man's life, if he is generous to God and faithful to grace, when the creatures that spoke so wonderfully of God will become silent; and the concepts that were like manna for his meditations will cease to feed his mind. It is here that God infuses into the soul a knowledge of Himself that is general and obscure but far superior to his own former clear and precise ideas of God. St. John of the Cross expresses it in these terms:

No thing, created or imagined, can serve the understanding as a proper means of union with God. All that the understanding can attain serves rather as an impediment [to this union] than as a means, if the soul should desire to cling to it. . . .

Among all created things, the things that belong to the understanding, there is no ladder whereby the understanding can attain to this High Lord. Rather it is necessary to know that if the understanding should seek to profit by all these things or by any of them as a proximate means of such union, they would be not only a hindrance, but even an occasion of numerous errors and delusions in the ascent of this mount.

To abandon this dark but sure way of contemplation, this "happy night," which the healthy, normal development of faith involves, would be to replace the real thing with a series of fabricated and human illusions. Did not our Lord say, according to St. John of the Cross: "I will lead thee by a way thou knowest not to the secret chamber of love"?

In faith there is only light; its obscurity is an effect of the transcendence of the light that shines upon the intellect when it searches into God and His Mystery.

When one is baptized God infuses faith into the soul. Whenever it is activated and exercised it grows. The practical question is then: how put this power of faith into action?

Thinking is the first way, since faith is rooted in the intellect. A vigorous, thoroughgoing intellectual life that is ruled by faith is the best introduction to a spiritual life. In fact, it is true to say that such an intellectual life is the spiritual life. Knowledge that is acquired by the intelligence, working in the human mode, has for St. John of the Cross all the validity it has for St. Thomas Aquinas. It penetrates in some sense all being. It achieves a valid univocal knowledge of created being, and it can truly know the supreme being of God with the aid of created analogies.

In the fifth stanza of the *Spiritual Canticle*, St. John speaks first of meditation upon creatures in all their wonder and variety, by which in the early states of the spiritual life, "the soul is greatly moved to love God." After all, is not God the most obvious fact of human experience? The world is crammed with God. So whenever a man thinks about God and divine things, he grows in faith.

The next way in which to make faith grow is by a daily program of *spiritual reading*. "On what meat doth this our Caesar feed that he has grown so strong?" We act the way we think; so much depends upon what gets into the mind. Faith must nourish itself on dogmatic truth. It cannot cling to God, it cannot enter upon its own proper domain of divine mystery, if the intelligence does not first adhere to the dogmatic formulas which express divine truth in human language. As Father Marie Eugene, O.C.D., points out in his excellent book, *I Want to See God,* "this nourishment of revealed truth is, in varying degrees, necessary to faith at every stage of its development but especially at the beginning. . . . Thus nourished by divine knowledge, faith grows strong and vigorous, it plumbs the depths of supernatural mysteries, rejoices in the splendors that shine in the formulas, while awaiting the purifying darkness that is to come, that will lead it into the yet more delectable savoring of divine truth as it is in itself."*

The necessity for such a consistent reading program is increased by the interrelated conditions of the human mind and the world. The intellect is surrounded by the open windows of the senses. And the world has concocted the most fantastic display of images, parading them endlessly before the windows of the soul. In order to withstand the deluge of these debilitating and distracting elements of the world, the mind must engage and occupy itself with Ultimate Reality—with the beauty, truth, and goodness of God.

Since there is such a paucity of time and energy in the average man's life, he must read discriminately. He must not miss the essential, the indispensable—and that is: the life of Christ, especially all of *pertinent* Scripture. I emphasize *pertinent* because there seems to be a moral compulsion on the part of many spiritual writers to urge the whole Bible on everyone. They can't really mean it!

Then the great classics of religious literature ought to be read, and most particularly, St. Teresa and St. John of the Cross. Only the best of contemporary writers should be read.

Thinking about God, knowing what creatures have to say about Him, studying the life of our Lord—this can never be enough. One never really gets to know Christ without *prayer.*

* Notre Dame, Ind.: Fides Publishers, 1953.

That is why our Lord directed that we should not merely watch, but "watch and pray. . . . Pray without ceasing." It is the difference between hearing all about a person and actually meeting him. The person met turns out to be much more than we had ever dreamed. Praying is meeting Christ. To pray is to know God by experience rather than by hearsay. To pray is to stand before the real Christ defenselessly, without hiding behind artificial barriers; it is to sit childlike, at the feet of Truth, and listen to Him, who "alone has the words of eternal life"; it is to converse with Him who loves us.

It is one thing to make isolated acts of faith; quite another to acquire the habit of making acts of faith. This is the function of prayer. It is an expression of faith; with repetition it becomes habitual: a man of prayer can live by faith, live always at least vaguely conscious of God's presence.

What happens when a man faithfully engages in a daily program of mental prayer? Information becomes conviction; an outline of Catholic faith becomes an experience; objective truth becomes a subjective, existential realization. Prayer is theology lived. God is a person, not just a three-letter word. The process of becoming human (a saint) is a process of falling in love. In mental prayer truth becomes excitingly interesting; Christ becomes progressively fascinating; God reveals Himself as He promised to do.

And that is why men of faith are haunted by His beauty ever ancient, ever new. They have one single reason for everything they do, and that reason is Christ.

We have seen how in the divine-human relationship it is always God who begins everything. We don't. We, for instance, cannot sanctify ourselves, we cannot make ourselves holy. We can become holy only if God sanctifies, and He does sanctify as we get to know Him and love Him. We cannot even begin to strive for our goals, for the possession of God, unless God takes the initiative, comes sweeping into our lives and gives us a push Godward. And that is the function of the theological virtue of hope.

Unfortunately, we don't hear much about hope; and today we need it more than ever before because we are living in an age of despair. We live in days that are shadowed by fear. There are, first of all, the private, personal fears, as there always have been: of failure, misunderstanding, and rejection; of pain, illness, and death; of the loss of those we love; of misfortune and tragedy striking close to home.

There is another kind of despair that creeps into a man's life in such a subtle, insidious way that he doesn't even recognize it; and without his knowing it, it eats away his heart and robs him of his best self. This is the kind of despair that tackles us in the middle of the day, in the middle of a job, or in the middle of a lifetime when all freshness, enthusiasm, and lyricism is gone, and life is nothing but a hard grind. We have hardly the will then, even to turn to Him who is our hope and salvation. How can we take Him our failures and frustrations if we lack the will to go to Him at all? Scripture calls this attack of despair "the noon-day devil." It ordinarily takes the form of boredom, monotony, drudgery. We are overcome by routine, by the ordinariness of life, by daily duties over and over again. So we take on a joyless, empty sort of quality which befits no Christian who should be the most sparkling and ebullient sort of person in the world, radiating the splendor and the glory of Christ in all the dark, dingy corners of the world.

This kind of despair is, perhaps, the most devastating and destructive because it goes unrecognized and, therefore, unchallenged. In the meantime, we are stultified by routine, induced into a rut, cease to be our best selves, and fail to conform to the living image of Christ that is within us, waiting only to unfold and be expressed.

Behind all these private fears there looms like a sinister backdrop the fear, anxiety, and misery of the world at large —universal cataclysmic despair: a relentless sense of foreboding, the inexorable feeling that disaster is imminent and will not be averted. Such fear from within a nation is a greater threat than the most formidable enemies without. For despair is, by definition, "the will-to-death." A nation gripped by despair destroys itself.

There is shocking evidence of this tragic form of despair in some statistics that point out the lamentable fact that during the Korean War as many men took their own lives at home, in America, as died in Korea. We average 16,000 suicides a year in America.

But there are three ways of committing suicide: killing oneself, letting oneself die, and letting oneself live. The last is the most common and in many ways the most pernicious type of suicide.

When fears are so dominating they make us gloomy, apathetic, uncreative, they make us forget God. And so we lose our zest for life, settle down into well-worn grooves of existence, become mediocre, complacent, and shorn of the stuff of human greatness.

The guilt of our age has begun to overwhelm us and now hangs in our nostrils like the stench of rotting flesh; it is corrupting our mind with the mass fear that comes of doubt and question; it is shriveling our hearts until they are like sheep for the slaughter; it is depriving us of the right to walk in forthright pride as men, destroying in us the brilliant heritage of God's image.

In this age of despair it is time for hope; time to preach it, write about it, pray for it, exercise it. Only the virtue of hope can combat despair, being the "will-to-life." That is why fear of any kind is not something simply to be escaped from, and as far as possible forgotten, but something to be faced, and understood, and transformed.

Modern man's despair is not despair of God at all, but despair of all that is not God. Beyond that despair lies Christian hope, the certainty that God alone is enough for man. In other words, hope in what God will make of man can grow out of despair at what man has made of man.

And so even such a tragic existentialist as Albert Camus is forced to say: "What we are all asked for, is words of hope." He goes on to say that the demand placed on our generation to despair is possibly a good preparation for talking of hope.

This is true. Modern man, having tasted despair, is more humanly disposed for a strong, unflinching hope—a hope without illusion and against escape, intolerant of rhetoric, bluff, and myth. But he must keep in proper perspective what Camus calls our "miserable and magnificent existence." There is always the danger of isolating either *man the magnificent* or *man the miserable*. The way to a balanced outlook is to speak of the "misery of man without God; the greatness of man with God."

Remember what another great Frenchman, Pascal, wrote:

The knowledge of God without that of man's misery causes pride. The knowledge of man's misery without that of God causes despair. The knowledge of Jesus Christ constitutes the middle course, because in Him we find both God and our misery.

So it is time for hope. But what is hope? It is a supernatural force in us: our share in divine power. It does not consist in an imperceptible extension of human expectations, and still less does it involve a strong element of naïveté; nor is it a superior kind of optimism. It is in a very real sense born in the soul; it is the fruit of a regeneration that has been achieved through the resurrection of the Savior.

Hope is that virtue which reaches out infinitely beyond human reach into the Kingdom of God, striving for what is apparently impossible and insuperable. Hope knows that life is too short to choose the second best. Hope makes us undertake arduous tasks for God. It scorns ease and comfort and thrives on difficulties. It knows that if great trials are avoided, great deeds also remain undone, and in hugging to a miserable sense of security, the possibility of nobleness is utterly lost.

We read in one of Sam Johnson's letters that:

To be without hope or fear, if it were possible, would not be happiness; it is better that life should struggle with obstructions, than stagnate and petrify. Never be without something to wish and something to do.

He also said that if you take the cross out of Christendom you make drab what ought to be dramatic. How true! Just imagine what would happen if we took away from mountain climbers the highest, most formidable peaks. Why, we would rob them of the sport, the exhilaration of mountain climbing. Take the hurdles out of a man's life and you leave him a dull, drab existence. We need to be challenged and provoked or else we become an apathetic, uninspiring people.

The first generation of Christians had a vivid anticipation of the world to come, but it slowly faded. Persecutions became less frequent. Christianity was first tolerated and later received official support, so that the world offered some Christians a superficial fulfillment of their hopes. Similarly, the fugitive priest in Graham Greene's *The Power and the Glory* succumbs to the magic of safety. When he has a brief respite from danger he comes close to falling back into what he was before his life was forfeit.

That is why Cardinal Newman said that "to be at ease is unsafe." And Pope Pius XI said that today, because of the terrible tensions of our age, it is no longer possible to be mediocre. We are forced to make a choice: to be heroes or cowards, hot or cold, with Christ or against Him.

A contemporary poet, Christopher Fry, was able to look out on the colossal chaos of our age, and, far from being discouraged, say:

Dark and cold we may be, but this
Is no Winter now. The frozen misery

Of centuries breaks, cracks, begins to move;
   The thunder is the thunder of the floes,
The thaw, the flood, the upstart Spring.
   Thank God our time is now when wrong
Comes up to face us everywhere,
   Never to leave us till we take
The longest stride of soul men ever took.
   Affairs are now soul size,
   The enterprise
   Is exploration into God.*

Hope is the boldest and most daring of all the virtues. It keeps the fires of ardor and enthusiasm burning brilliantly in the hearts of youthful people. It is only when little people, children, dwell too long and too frequently with dull, drab adults that they lose their selfhood, their creativity and uniqueness, their boldness, daring, and their hope.

When you cease to be a child you cease to be yourself; you are already dead. Today it is extremely difficult to be oneself. The pressures of society are against it; they are much more conducive to commonplace instincts, gregariousness, sameness, and mediocrity.

"Unless you become as little children, you cannot enter the Kingdom of Heaven." We begin heaven on earth to the extent that we are striving, living by hope. Hope is the condition of our existence as knowing subjects, a condition that by its very nature cannot be fixed: it is neither comprehension and possession nor simply nonpossession, but "not-yet-possession." We are given eternal life. The unique and thrilling thing about this gift is that it is both present and future; and so we can take full joy in the present and still be full of expectation.

A man of hope is a man of desire. If there are few saints in the world it is because few men have desired sanctity. Everything in our lives depends upon what we desire. We become what we desire. If we desire nothing more than a Thunderbird, we become a Thunderbird. If we desire success, we become success, an abstract and irrational sort of

* Christopher Fry, *A Sleep of Prisoners,* last act. (New York: Oxford University Press, Inc.), p. 47.

thing. If we desire prosperity, money, comfort, we become all these things personified; but we also become heartless, heedless, and inhuman. We become great big zeros. If we desire God, we become God by participation. In other words, we share His divinity; we share His Godhead; we share His knowledge, love, and life all because, fundamentally, we desire Him above all other things.

Our big job, then, begins every morning when we wake up and all sorts of weird, fantastic desires come rushing at us like wild animals. Then and there we've got to push them all back and be very selective and discriminating. Those that fit into the great-souled desire for God can be brought in. But those that oppose God, compete with Him, that drive God out of mind and heart—they've got to be ruthlessly rooted out. Nothing is lost and all is gained. Once we possess God we possess everything else all at once because God is, in a sense, everything else all at once. We see and love and possess the manifold in the One.

To live by hope is to lean on God and expect everything from His mercy. What is the foundation of such great hope? The fact that we have been *christened*. It is to know that we are weak but God is strong; that God has chosen the weak to confound the strong; that God lives in us, we live in Him and wield His power. Through Him we can do all things.

Jacques Maritain paraphrasing the parables of the man counting his resources before building a tower, and the king counting his army before meeting his enemy in the field, says:

A man of hope, then, does not count on his own human strength or his own individual effort; neither does he *presume* that God will save him despite his reckless life. Every man needs to be buoyed up and carried on by a life greater than his own. Every man needs to know and rely on the fact that he is a member of the Whole Christ, the Mystical Body of Christ. There are times, in fact, when a man believes and hopes with the faith and hope of others. When his own grip slackens he is supported by the community. When he is discouraged he leans on the hope of the people of God, the communion of saints.

It is, above all, a man's friendship with Christ that enables him to hope so daringly. "Have confidence in Me, for I have overcome the world." He has risen from the dead and even now prepares a place in heaven for those who love Him.

Although Christianity is very much taken up with readying us for the next world, it does not neglect or disdain this world. It is the business of Christianity not only to interpret this world against the background of eternity, but to change the world. Christianity doesn't have to be modernized or modified for the task; but it does have to be taken seriously and lived. G. K. Chesterton said that even watered-down Christianity could boil all modern society to rags.

Our Christian longing for heaven does not diminish our Christian love of this world. We are responsible for the world. We cannot seek our own salvation and ignore the rest of men. The more conscious we are of our citizenship in heaven, the more we respect that world in which our heavenly citizenship began. Before we are a Church of triumph and glory we are a militant Church—a Church of birth and painful, uneven growth, a Church that reproduces itself. We, the members of that Church, must, here and now, build the city of man and dispose it for the coming of Christ in glory. There is hardly anything we pray for so much: "Thy Kingdom come. Thy will be done on earth as it is in heaven."

The man of hope must be a man of *action*—restless, alert, apostolic. We are guilty of inertia when we refuse to give ourselves to temporal endeavors on the ground that we belong to eternity. For instance, to accept inhuman living conditions as normal because we know that our Lord will "make it up to us" in the next world is to vitiate the meaning of the Gospels.

An intelligent and sincere Christian knows that every improvement of life and every attempt to increase the earth's beauty and fruitfulness spring from charity, justice, and hope.

Such a Christian knows that social reform is a duty that endures as long as human society. All things must be restored in Christ. This requires on the part of the Christian constant re-forming of society and himself. The Church enters a society to transform it. This it has done and will continue to do mysteriously, inventively, infallibly. For the Church is God working through history; and we can attribute to the Church what we say of God:

They shall perish, but thou shalt continue; and they shall grow old as a garment and as a vesture shalt thou change them and they shall be changed; but thou art the self-same and thy years shall not fail (Heb 1:11–12).

Philosophers and theologians have come closest to the reality and the scriptural references to it when they expressed the divine-human romance in terms of bridegroom and bride. The preliminaries of the great marriage between heaven and earth belong to God alone. It is up to the bridegroom to make the first advances. Nothing man does can compare with the unbounded liberality, the reckless, ravishing initiative of God's first love.

Good tends naturally toward self-diffusion. This conclusion of philosophy and experience (think how magnanimous, good-natured, selfless people give themselves unsparingly to others) has its perfect verification in God. God would not keep His goodness to Himself and the sharing of it was creation. We were not only created out of love, but we exist out of love. God's love continually creates us. Each one of us is the complete and total object of God's attentive love. If God would cease to love me even for a moment, I would cease to be, I would disintegrate, fall back into nothingness. I get all of God's love. It is as if I were the only one in the whole world drinking in the whole of God's infinite, personal love for me. It is as if you were the only object of His love. And this is true of all the other millions of us. God does not have to divide up His love.

Whatever happens in a lifetime has been planned and decreed from all eternity by a God of love because of love. If we could grasp this most real thing in our lives, if we could anchor our lives in this immutable reality, we would always be serene, always enthusiastic, always in control of every situation, no matter how appalling or dreadful.

The supreme instance of God's love is contained in the Incarnation of the Second Person of the Blessed Trinity. "For God so loved the world as to give his only-begotten Son: that whosoever believeth in him may not perish, but may have life everlasting." This is the epiphany of God, the burn-

ing and glowing of Him right in the camp of man. This is
God in His most attractive form. Christ has stolen all the radi-
ant splendor and glory of the Godhead and made it manifest
to us. This is the supreme act of divine love: that He should
share with us the intimate secrets of the Godhead, of trinitarian life, the family life of God. He lived a life on earth so
captivatingly lovable it is enough to tear the heart out of any
human being, and turn his own life inside out like a glove.
"And greater love than this no man has than to lay down his
life for a friend"; and so the God of heaven and earth laid
it down to prove once and for all that He loves us.

The Incarnation is God's final message to mankind; it is
such a full, rich message overflowing with love that its complete significance will not be realized until the end of time,
but essentially there is nothing more to add. God has spoken
His Word, His Word was made flesh, and His gospel name
is Love.

God loves, hounds, pursues, entices, woos. All that half-
awakened, utterly dependent, fragile, sinful little man can do
is respond and abandon himself to God's cascading glory, His
devastating demands, His consuming fire of love. Out of his
response, his uncompromising surrender to absolute love,
man achieves his wholeness, that is, his holiness, his perfection.

Such a whole response is required of us: "You are to be
perfect, as your heavenly Father is perfect." Christ said that
without equivocation or reservation of any kind; said it just
as seriously as when, on another occasion, He said: "This is
my Body and this is my Blood." And it was a command to all
to be perfect, not as saints or angels, but as God is perfect—
not the same degree of divine perfection but the same kind.
This, of course, does not oblige us to be perfect here and
now, but it does oblige us today and tomorrow and tomorrow to be in the pursuit of perfection; that is, to desire it
efficaciously, to aim at it daily, to fix our will on it.

If goals are going to be attainable, they've got to be seen
or conceptualized as clearly as possible. Perfection, then,
must not be a vague, general sort of notion. It must be understood as precisely and scientifically as possible. St. Thomas

says that a thing is perfect when it fulfills the purpose for which it was created. For instance, a knife is perfect when it cuts cleanly; a gun is perfect when it shoots accurately. A man is perfect when he achieves the purpose for which he was created: union with God. Once we discover what it is that unites a man to God we know what it is that perfects him—and that is love: "he who abides in love abides in me and I in him."

When our love of God is perfect we are perfect. That is how simple the spiritual life is. That is why complicated lives are so unspiritual, and so unnecessary. Our lives must be permeated, motivated, and crowned by charity. Everything else in our lives—the virtues, the rules, the ritual, etc.—are valuable and significant only to the extent that they either cause, intensify, or preserve love. Love is the whole law.

That is why St. John of the Cross said that at the end of life we will be judged by love; not by achievements and successes, but by love; not by what we did so much as with how much love we did it. He also said that one act of pure love of God is worth far more than all sorts of other activity put together. That is why you cannot judge apostolic fruitfulness by external activity alone. A bedridden woman may be more apostolic than a hustling, bustling missionary. Washing dishes may, in this sense, be more vital than preaching a sermon. And so St. Francis de Sales insisted that a snap of the finger done with two ounces of love is worth more than martyrdom done with only one ounce of love. It is probably harder to live for Christ than to die for Him, anyway. It means dying daily to the false self. It means performing all the ordinary daily tasks with extraordinary love. And that is the greatest kind of heroism; that is the stuff of sanctity.

Now, since charity is of the essence of perfection, the practical question is how do we grow in the love of God? We must begin by indicating a distinction of the highest importance. There are two kinds of love of God. One is natural: the tendency by which the will goes out toward God insofar as He is known as the Creator and Author of nature. The other is supernatural: the love of God as He is known by revelation in His intimate nature. This kind of supernatural love—the kind we are concerned with here—would be beyond the powers of man except for Christ. Here was the one Man —the only Man—full of charity, full of the Holy Spirit. This is equally true of His Mystical Body as it was of His physical body. If we want to get warm we've got to get near the fire, if we want to get wet we've got to get into the water; and so if we want to possess and grow up in the love of God we've got to get into the unique source of supernatural and divine love, into the one person in the world who is full of charity, full of the Holy Spirit.

So it is by getting into and growing up in Christ—thinking like Him, loving like Him, and acting like Him, being transformed into Him that we learn to love God. This whole process of transformation in love is initiated and effected by the liturgy, begun in baptism when we are incorporated into Christ, and culminated in the Eucharist, the Sacrament of love, of union.

But within the objective framework of the liturgy, incessant, personal, subjective effort of loving God is required. First of all we need to develop a personal, intimate knowledge of God because we cannot love what we do not know. This means that we need to do some deep thinking, good reading, real meditating—and for this we need copious supplies of silence, solitude, and mental prayer, as well as continuous effort to live as consciously as possible in the presence of God.

Knowledge, however, is not love. Thinking about God, hearing about Him, knowing Him is not yet loving Him. And so it is vastly important to learn to love God by loving Him. It may be that in a given moment we are capable of only a spark of love; but unless that spark is fanned by the exercise of love into a strong flowing flame, it will remain a spark or, even worse, go out. And so we learn to love God by loving Him on good days and bad days, when we are bright and gay as well as when we are dull and troubled.

The greatest expression and proof of love of God is, always, sacrifice. This way we prove by deeds that we prefer God to everything else. If I am hungry, I am perfectly willing to give up a quarter for a loaf of bread, thus proving that at this moment I prefer—love—the bread more than the money. It is not as if I gave up anything. I exchanged. And that is the meaning of sacrifice. Our Lord said: "trade till I come"; exchange temporal things for eternal, human for divine, everything for God.

Learning to love God means learning to love His world. God is something like the proud parent who says, "Love me, love my child." God says, "Love Me, love My world." Perfect love of God does not mean that we love nothing but God; it means that we love all in God. Christian love involves responsibility for the whole world and everyone and everything in it. It means the Christian ought to be full of deep concern and solicitude for all because he is a lover of God and His creation. I think one of the best expressions of love I know is a Buddhist prayer: "May all creatures be happy."

Of all creatures the one for whom we are most responsible is man himself, God's masterpiece, God's own image and likeness. This business of loving one's fellow man is, in fact, the supreme means of growing in the love of God, that is, ultimately, the final, acid test of whether or not we really love God at all. "He who says he loves God and hates his brother is a liar." Since this is the central proving ground of love we are going to consider it quite thoroughly.

The command to love one another requires that we desire efficaciously the well-being of another, no matter how we feel. To desire this efficaciously means to use whatever is at our disposal to make this desire come as close to realization as possible. This is the barest kind of love; this much at least we are obliged to do under the pain of sin. We must achieve much more than the minimal requirements of fraternal charity.

Love is an activity. I don't mean our modern, emasculated idea of activity: moving things from one place to another. But when we mention "activity," that is the sort of thing that comes to mind. We are impressed by the enormous achievements of our practical skill at moving things about, and so we are inclined to the foolish notion that love is out of this world and has nothing to do with and even threatens the important worldly business of living. We assume that to en-

gage for very long in the activity of love—dwelling in the
holy—is a wasteful substitute for doing the work of the world.
And so we get caught up in a frenzy of profane worldliness—
high-pressure salesmanship, power politics, inducing a man
to do this, making a woman do that, exploiting and capitaliz-
ing, using men as mere hands, climbing over others into
grandeur, stealing the show, getting ahead, walking away
with the prizes.

What a caricature of activity! So Ecclesiastes exclaimed
upon the vanity of doing; and Thomas Hardy asked the
dreary question: "Why do I go on doing what I do, and not
cease?" To love is *to be:* a much more vital and robust kind
of activity than that required to do. To love is to dwell in
the holy before we do, while we do, and after we have done.
To love sanctifies our lives in the real world and our doing
in the moment of doing it. Love is not apart from the world or
above the world, but the only way of fulfilling our lives in
the world. There is no whole communion with the present,
with the world, with one another, and with God except by
way of love.

A man is a response to God; and the first work of man is
by way of love to stand on holy ground in being that response. Only there in holy leisure, under God's holy scrutiny
can we meet one another and know the world. This is real.
Without this reality all our doing is but a sickness unto death.

When a man is driven by ambition, greed, and money to
labor at medicine, engineering, or sports he is not active at
all but passive; he is the sufferer not the actor. But when he
contemplates—gives long, loving attention to things as they
are—he engages in the highest activity there is, an activity
of the soul which is possible only under the condition of inner
freedom and independence.

So love is not a passive effect, it is an activity; it is not a
"falling for," but a "standing in." It is not an appetite, but
a value response par excellence. Love is the whole response
of one person to the beauty and worth of the individuality
of another person. And on the supernatural level this beauty
and truth can always be affirmed in terms of faith and in
reference to Christ. In order to love a person, the true design

of God, which is made incarnate in the individual, must illumine for us his entire beauty and worth. In the most general way, the active character of love can be described by stating that love is primarily giving, not receiving.

The lover gives not for the sake of suffering, deprivation, or sacrifice, but for the sake of the beloved. The lover does not make the common mistake of thinking that it is always better to suffer deprivation than to experience joy. Giving is the highest expression of potency. In the very act of giving, a man experiences his own strength, wealth, power. This experience of heightened vitality and potency fills him with joy—the joy of overflowing, the spending of being very much alive. Giving is more joyous than receiving, not because it impoverishes a man, but because, in the act of giving, a man comes most alive.

Rich men are capable of giving material things. The richest man in the world is the one capable of giving himself. He can confer of himself to others. He gives of his very life, of his joy, of his sadness, of his interest, of his understanding, of his wit—of what is most alive in him. Although his giving is a self-oblivious donation, he cannot help but receive that which is given back to him. Love produces love and is, therefore, reciprocated. If a lover, by his donation of so much life, does not become a loved person, then his love is impotent. Even if one participates in the life of the other, in his thoughts, plans, etc., so long as the loved one does not reciprocate and turn his spiritual countenance toward him, the longed-for union cannot be fulfilled. In so many ways, giving means receiving. As Erich Fromm says: "The teacher is taught by his students, the actor is stimulated by his audience, the psychoanalyst is cured by his patient—provided they do not treat each other as subjects, but are related to each other genuinely and productively."*

We have said that love is the supreme human activity. If so, then it is also great labor. The choice to love is the highest achievement of man's will, and the good hard work of loving is man's proper spiritual toil. If we shirk this, all else

* *Art of Loving* (New York: Harpers, 1956), pp. 25–26.

we do is futile. The far-flung, massy, and pretentious work of the world is trivial compared to the work of love, which is a divine employment: to work and be and live with God.

It is hard work. Each time we choose to love, we endanger our way of living. Ease, comfort, security, survival—a veritable routine of false gods—are wrecked when met head-on with love. When we who love offer our lives at full risk we shake the foundations of our way of living.

We hate loneliness but are still afraid to love. How many shifts and dodges we use to be left untouched and untouchable, all alone. We speak of the incomparable glory of friendship but prefer to be uncommitted, uninvolved. How often we hide behind masks and hug delusions with compulsive passion because we are afraid to be known, to be loved—but in the nearness of real, deep, substantial love we run back to our masks of isolation, shallowness, and safety in terror of being revealed and accepted. We hide ourselves in acts of passion; we bury love under false prudence; we substitute biological pleasures for the divine wonder and peril of love; we surround ourselves with cold, icy barriers to defend the smug self from being shattered by love.

It is easier to snub another ("snuff the light of his life out of our life") than to love. And so we indulge in spiritual assassination in order to protect our own convenience. It is easier to love humanity than to love the individual man. If we have not begun love at home, any pretension we make about loving the whole of mankind is but empty twaddle. To champion mankind around the globe is to appear great but to be in fact small if we avoid the true work of loving any real person here and now. Communication with the world at large means very little if there is no real communion, face to face, at home.

It takes courage to love. It is the supreme fulfillment of human courage, for we have to overcome all the enemies of love which are so plentiful, subtle, and insidious: pride, fear, self-complacency, softness, human respect, ignorance, etc. Love is an intentional act of illuminated wisdom.

There is grief and sorrow in love, too. But it is worth keeping love alive in the world. Think of what God said through

St. John the Evangelist: "He who abides in love abides in me and I in him." Refuse to love and you kill the presence of God and the meaning of life. We are guilty of that. We burden our days with a thousand little murders: the spiritual murders of the vicious word, the cold glance, the smug attitude, the snobbish decision, carelessness, callousness, and segregation. When we say that a man has got to look after himself and fight for his rights, we are really offering a thin and fatuous apology for the blank face and cold shoulder with which we go about our daily killing of the tender and merciful presence of God.

The active quality of love is characterized by certain elements named by Fromm as care, responsibility, respect, and knowledge.

Love is the active concern for the life and the growth of that which we love. A mother proves her love of her children only if she diligently, anxiously cares for them. A man really loves his flowers only if he cultivates them with delicate and dexterous attention. We are to be full of concern for one another. This is the positive part of the commandment of love. It is not enough to avoid hurting a neighbor by word or deed; we are obliged to care for him with intelligent and warm-hearted love; to inspire him, to cherish him, to cheer and buoy him up, to defend him, to help him.

Human life is a response to reality. To be able and willing to respond to another human being is to be "responsible." As Christians we are responsible for the whole world: "All things are yours, you are Christ's, and Christ is God's." There is no such thing as an isolated Christian. "No man is an island." None of us may say: I am going to take care of my own destiny and let the world go hang. We must be acutely, poignantly alive to the needs and interests of our fellowmen.

We don't fulfill responsibility by throwing our weight around. We must not become possessive and domineering busybodies. Coupled, therefore, with responsibility must be respect. *Respicere* means "to look at." And when we have a steady, deep look at a person we see him as he is: a unique, distinct, unrepeatable creation, an image and likeness of God, one for whom Christ died, the most mysterious thing in the world. The person is therefore accepted and responded to as he is, that is, ontologically good, true, and beautiful. And so in the presence of something so fundamentally sacred—even though defective and unpleasant on the surface level—we stand in awe and reverence eschewing curt criticism and refusing to exploit or even to ignore.

But we cannot really respect a person unless we know him. We cannot love what we do not know. But neither can we know what we do not love. The one who loves is the one who really knows and understands. Chesterton said that things deceive us by being more real than they seem. One who loves gets through the periphery, through the external features into the "more real," into the "freshness-deep-down things," into the innermost secret of a man.

It happens every time the writer conducts a retreat: at the opening conference he beholds a crowd of commonplace, ordinary, unimpressive faces. At the closing conference every single face is to him an exquisitely beautiful thing. Why? There was no change in them. But there was in him: between the opening and the closing conferences he spent his time and energy with them in a work of love and came to know them and found them lovable. Man is not a thing. We don't force his secret out. It takes the long, costly, active penetration of love, the interpenetration of persons. In the act of fusion we know him, and we are known. We know each other by experience—the experience of union. That is why it is always a mistake to make pat judgments, perfunctory statements, harsh and peremptory criticisms. We must wait, look, explore, work respectfully, and then respond with the wholeness of love to the wholeness of reality.

A "real," natural, burning love of a human being is compatible with a true love of God. Christ fills the whole self and not only the soul. It is the whole person that is touched by God's triune, personal love. With a really great love it is not hard to think of the blood catching fire from the white-hot soul. And so it is deleterious to attempt to divest charity of its true character of love, thinking that the less the heart—the feelings—partake of fraternal charity, the more perfect and pleasing to God it is. Love for Christ's sake is interpreted

in somewhat the following way: I am completely indifferent
to this man, but for Christ's sake I will be good to him. This
is acting as if one loved the other—and it's not the good "as
if" principle that leads to reality; it's the bad kind—hypocrisy
—that takes the place of reality. The command of Christ,
however, has to do with interior dispositions: we should possess a much greater, more intense and passionate interest in
the neighbor if we love him for Christ's sake. To love for
Christ's sake does not mean to turn to Him over the head
of one's own neighbor, but rather to perceive the neighbor
in his ultimate significance whence we find and love Christ
in him and share in the love of Christ for him. When we do
this we fulfill the new command of the Lord which He gave
us: "that we love one another as he loved us." Is Christ's love
a thin, pallid, neutral love? Is that what we think, what we
want?

Love of God and neighbor becomes for some a cold, dutiful thing because they think of it in terms of an act of obe-
dience, nothing more. And they defend themselves with the
words of Scripture: "Whoever keeps my commands, he it is
who loves me." These words of our Lord by no means justify
the identification of love and pure will. Keeping the commandments is indeed the test, the criterion, of the reality and
sincerity of our love; but it is not the whole thing. True, God
requires no more than that we try, as best we can, painfully
and stumblingly to do His will. But we must not dismiss the
problem too lightly by turning the truth that a good will is
sufficient, into an exaggeration that it is the only right attitude, and everything beyond that unimportant, mere decora-
tive trappings.

Feeling is often excessively ignored, unduly denigrated. It
is confused with sentimentality, and regarded as a vapid,
sweet froth, a temperamental indulgence or pleasure in love
which a serious-minded man whose love is a matter of will,
neither needs nor desires. Emotion is a worthy and indispensable part of the human response. It is a vital force which
the will needs if it is to catch fire and not remain only "the
will to love," but become actually love. And so Ida Goerres
says: "There is, then, emotion of great power, of high quality,

of profound depth, of creative energy. With all its bliss such love can be one of the heaviest, most painful burdens one can carry; a charge on our whole energy, full of tension, of fear and trembling, of problems and claims, of deepest earnest and melancholy, of anxiety and reverence."

Love of neighbor, therefore, as well as love of God, is not purely a matter of will, chill to the core, directed by common sense. It is "real" love—a response of the whole man: intelligent, strong, vital, passionate, dangerous. St. Therese's growth in holiness did not incline her to love her family less but more. St. Elizabeth's love of God did not lessen her love of husband or deprive her of the pain of parting or the anguished longing and unappeasable loneliness in her husband's absence. St. Joan of Arc loved God but did not, because of that, love her soldiers or her horses less.

In fact, it's quite the other way around. To love the neighbor for Christ's sake is nothing less than a participation in Christ's love for our neighbor. Lacordaire says: *"Il n'y a pas deux amours, l'un celeste et l'autre terrestre; ce n'est qu'un seul sentiment avec la différence que l'un est infinis."** He does not mean to do away with the distinction between natural and supernatural love. He means that what is found in natural love, as the essence of love and its life force is not lost but rather is subsumed by supernatural power and expressed in a more excellent way.

This is so true that every love—love of a child, of parents, of a friend, marital love—becomes a betrayed and crippled love as long as it remains purely natural and is not transformed and transfigured in Christ. In Him alone can love of friend, spouse, parent, child reach its final satisfaction and fulfillment. Every relationship which is transformed in Christ glorifies God, because in a mysterious manner it is informed, molded, and animated by the love of God.

* "There are not two loves, one heavenly and the other earthly; it is but one sentiment, with the difference that the one is infinite."

The life of man is meant to be a personal response to a personal God. To respond to God means to be alive to God. Being alive to God involves knowing and loving; raised to the highest pitch of awareness, it is contemplation. With original sin man lost the knack of contemplating God, ceased to respond adequately to His infinite love, and suffered an acute rupture in his divine relationship. Sinful man thus became irreversibly separated from the unique and sovereign source of life. He and his children were doomed to a life of death.

Religion is the *way* back to God. It is the way by which man returns to life (and "this is eternal life; that you may know God and Jesus Christ whom he has sent"). It is the way man relearns to contemplate. It is the way by which God is announced and presented to man; the way through which man's devotion and love goes to God. The word "way" is emphasized to accentuate the fact that religion is in danger whenever it ceases to be a *way,* whenever movement ceases, coming to a standstill in the work itself.

Religion, then, is both the way that God arranges for our rebirth and reunion, and the way we manage to respond and worship—recognize and proclaim His "worth"—in spirit and in truth. I shall refer to God's arrangement as the *structure of religion* and to *our* inspired efforts toward response (contemplation) as the *virtue of religion.*

The New Testament's affirmation that it was God's "loving design, centered in Christ, to give history its fulfillment by resuming everything in him, all that is in heaven, all that is on the earth, summed up in him" (Eph. 1:9–10), is a statement of unparalleled significance. Jesus Christ in His very person is religion incarnate. He reunited man to God by being Himself the bridge, the mediator between heaven and earth.

Man could not lift himself up out of his own cellar of sin, his own confinement of time and place, and enter a relationship with Christ. The Savior had to enter into man's existential situation and create a new relationship to God. God alone rescues us from our nothingness, from the absurdity of our insoluble human condition. Christ alone gives meaning to man's time and place in being, through faith and the sacraments. As St. Thomas expresses it: "Although Christ's passion is corporal, from its unity with the divinity, it possesses a spiritual power. And therefore it obtains its efficacy through spiritual contact, i.e., through faith and the sacraments of faith."

Now that in His person a totally new link has been forged between God and man, a totally new response of the human spirit to the demands of the divine becomes appropriate. Christ Himself is the first manifestation of the incarnational or sacramental principle in religion. The material, the finite, the human is made sacred by the choice of God; it becomes a means of contact and union of man with God; it lifts men up to God and no longer casts them far from Him. The Preface of the Christmas Mass tells it delightfully: "Through Him, whom we know by sight, we are drawn to love of things invisible." The theology of the sacraments uses the same theme; for sensible things, as water, bread, oil, and human words, become the signs and carriers of divine grace to man.

The nature which groaned and travailed until the advent of the God-Man is now made holy for him and all things are drawn with him to Christ, as He promised. Man is no longer enslaved to Satan, and his place in creation no longer alienates him from God above and inferior natures below, and his moment in time no longer slips from the meaningless past to the meaningless future.

The mediatorship of Christ is still alive in the world. The Church is Christ. It prolongs His incarnation and thus makes it possible for our Lord to continue His mediatorship *in person*. Religion is the way (the sacramental way) this incalculable Person sets the stage and creates the proper environment for both the disclosure of the unfathomable mystery of the Godhead, "kept secret from all eternity," and the adequate response of the needy, hungry, half-awakened little human creature.

Man's personal encounter with a living God is the ultimate reason for *all* religious beliefs, duties, obligations, and ceremonies. It is of capital importance to keep this final end of religion in mind; for there is a very real danger of making a fetish of liturgical maneuvers and of sacrificing prayer to performance.

Through Baptism man's life is reorientated, his nature reformed and dignified; his past is corrected and his future assured. Through Confirmation God enters more deeply into man's inner world, heightens and enriches his social life, confirming him in his faith and giving him the duty and privilege of radiating Christ with apostolic vigor.

Christ rearranged things, making some things so sacred that they have become the channels of His divine life to man as well as the instruments of our human response, our worship. But He did more than that. He gave Himself as our way back to God. "I am the Way. . . . He who sees me sees the Father."

This vastly important aspect of the liturgy is rather sadly neglected: seeing the Father—this is heaven, this is eternal life, this is contemplation. And this is what we are meant to achieve even now through a religion of faith and the sacraments. Faith gives us the power to see; and the sacraments give us something (Someone) to see.

Religion, then, must announce; it must prepare the way for the sacred *image of Christ* which speaks to the believer out of the memory of the Church.

We have no document which speaks of Jesus purely from the viewpoint of history. And if we did, it would have no more relevance or value than a photograph. The portrait we do have of Christ is based on a faithful, accurate reminiscence, a reminiscence fathered by the Holy Spirit. This inspired memory of the Church attains the Son of God in reality, with eyes capable of seeing the Lord and a mind capable of understanding His message. The image of Christ took shape in the reminiscence of an Apostle as such, invested with the role of laying bare the portrait of the Lord. This

Apostle—Matthew, for instance—was not a private individual but a bishop of the Church. It was in virtue of the authority which he possessed in the Church that he evoked his memories and proclaimed them. And so it is precisely the memory of the Bridegroom, of the Church, that provides for us the only reliable portrait of Christ. Even the Gospels are just a part—an extremely important part—of the memory of the Church.

This true image is a living thing with its immutable core in the Incarnation and Redemption; but its character changes. Even among the Evangelists there are differences of nuance and tone. But all of them give us one objective Christ, the unique embodiment of God, to contemplate.

Christ Himself, then, is the Mystery which is seen by angels, and "believed in the world." Yet Christ has been seen in the world too, and therefore faith is not incompatible with every form of "sight." Does the Ascension of Christ into glory mean that men have been deprived of this epiphany, this "shining forth of God"? The Church assures us that this is not so, for not only has Christ our God been seen from Christmas to Ascension by thousands of men whose bodies have gone to the dust long ago, but He is seen today: "Visibly we see God," says the Christmas Preface. So there is something even now to rejoice our hearts.

Where can we see Him? In the "breaking of bread," as did the disciples of Emmaus. St. Leo said: "What was visible in our Redeemer has now passed into mysteries."

To repeat and sum up this capital point about the structure of religion: The Word was made flesh, thus becoming for us the absolute Image of God. Christ is the Sign of God, and it is because He signifies God in a visible, tangible way. He is no less seen and no less known by men in the twentieth century than by the disciples of the first.

That is why the liturgical movement should not overlook or play down the "memorial" aspect of the Eucharist. "Do this in memory of me," our Lord commanded. And so one of the vastly important things we do in the liturgy is reminisce about Christ. St. Teresa of Avila is often cited as an ardent exponent of the liturgy. But why she was such an enthusiast is not ordinarily added. It was precisely because the liturgy managed to focus her mind on the Lord. "All of our trouble comes," she said, "from not keeping our eyes on Him."

Teresa appreciated the God-centered, objective piety of the liturgy; but she was also rightfully concerned that liturgical prayer have a strong, vital, subjective effect on herself and her Sisters.

Some liturgical enthusiasts (incidentally, the author is a liturgical enthusiast) err by an insufficient penetration of the *finis creationis*. We so often hear it presented with an unfortunate slant: God cannot gain any internal glory, but before creation He lacked external glory. So He created to get it.—That is a distortion. The Vatican Council did define that the world was created for His glory, but a study of the acts shows they mean it as *finis operis*, not *finis operantis*. Really, God acts like a father. A father does not say to himself: I want to have children so that I may have someone to honor me. It is true, he wants children to do so, but for two reasons: (1) because objective goodness and right demand that children honor their parent or Creator; (2) because if they refuse, they make themselves indisposed to receive his favors, which he, in supreme love and generosity wishes to give.

Now, to put so much stress on objective piety, ignoring how it may or may not benefit the individual who worships, *could* imply a feeling that God wants most of all that we pay "objective" honor, even when and in ways in which it is not for our good. This would partially separate our good and His glory—which are, by His generous will, inseparable. Every Father as such seeks His honor through the good of His children. It is His glory that they fare well. Hence God adapts Himself to us, in the principle of *providential diversity*. And even on the objective plane, whatever promotes the private spiritual good of the individual, contributes to objective improvement, for the individual is part of the mystical Christ. The Head is always perfect, the members not so. Whatever perfects the members, helps the perfection of the offering in its objectivity much more than does an improvement in the external mode.

Religion, considered *as a moral virtue*, is a perfection of the will disposing us to acknowledge dutifully the absolute supremacy of God, the unique source from whence all our good proceeds. The religious disposition inclines us to worship God, that is to say: to recognize, affirm, and respond to the infinite "worth" of God. It ranks first among the moral virtues because it deals more directly with God than all the others. Its function is to reunite man with God through manly things—things of the world, of the flesh, of matter. It has less dignity than the theological virtues which relate man directly to God. Religion is much more taken up with the honor and glory of God than with God Himself.

The *structure* of religion makes an adequate response to God's love possible. The *virtue* of religion makes the response whole and correct.

The human response is primarily a man's prayer. "Prayer," says St. Thomas, "is the activity of religion." This activity of religion is what we refer to when we speak of *liturgy:* the prayer of Christ passing through the lips of the Church, the public, official prayer of the Whole Christ, head and members. This liturgical life of the Church, expressed through the sacramental system, especially the Mass, is what Pope Pius X referred to as the "primary and indispensable source of the true Christian spirit." And that is why since then there has been a wholesome and consistent papal insistence upon intelligent, active participation in the liturgy.

The plea of the popes has not been an invitation to all Christians to become liturgical aesthetes, rubricists, activists, or missal mice, but to become authentic liturgists, that is: men or women who come, by the way they know best, to be identified and equated with Christ the perfect High Priest of creation and Victim of love. They are, in other words, people who are governed by a genuine spirit of prayer.

Liturgy keeps the prayer human: an intelligent expression of the whole man directed properly to God. It sees to it that all things "made sacred" are incorporated, that intellect and will are properly fed, that the senses are stimulated, and, finally, that Scripture and Tradition are the chief sources for the content of prayer. Religion also regulates and assures the true hierarchy of prayer: it inspires and fosters adoration, thanksgiving, reparation, and petition—in more or less that order. It prevents man's prayer from becoming self-centered, sentimental, pietistic, and too individualistic.

The particular scope of religion should by now be obvious. With a great deal of careful regulation and a keen sense of propriety and an uncanny knack of handling things, religion readies a man for contemplation, for the personal encounter with the living God, for divine union through the "intense" exercise of the theological virtues of faith, hope, and charity.

The word "intense" is in bas-relief to indicate the fact that the theological virtues have been in action along with religion but their activity becomes intense (and thus transforming) only in conjunction with contemplation.

Let me attempt to explain the function of the virtue of religion in another way—a limping, faltering, homely way, but perhaps clarifying.

Religion is like a prim, proper, social-minded woman who says: "Let's have a party and invite the men." She selects the right place, arranges things properly: the seating, the furniture, the ornaments, the flowers. She sees that the guests are received courteously, introduced properly, and entertained appropriately. That's her function: to make the party "go." So far so good. She's indispensable and everyone loves her.

But she spoils the whole thing—this gay lady, this charming, easy-to-look-at, unendurable bore—when she does more than she should; when she becomes inordinately fussy and fastidious; when she insists on keeping everyone busy; when she says: "Never let two men sit together or they'll get talking about some subject and then there'll be no fun."

Her point could not have been more accurately made. Talk, by all means; the more of it the better; unceasing cascades of the human voice; but not, please, a deep, engaging subject. "And don't let those young couples out under the stars; this is no time for loving. The party must keep moving. We're *all* going to cut the cake together in a few minutes so don't go away." Dreadful old lady! And so religion is always doing *something* and arranging *things*, creating the atmosphere, the mood, and filling the place with the right articles:

music, men, manners, ceremony, food, pictures, statues, and talk.

But, just as the woman who decided on a party, religion's scope is limited. It is, as put down before, a *way*. All this endless prattling, hustle and bustle, and "jolly" must not replace or eclipse the deep, manly, robust intercourse of minds that ought to happen quite readily at good parties. And religion—even the most full-bodied, splendid, dashing liturgical performance—should not interfere with the divine-human encounter; it should, in fact, set it up.

Religion cannot be genuine without devotion. Devotion, the will to give oneself steadily to God, is an act of the virtue of religion. Devotion is inspired by God but it is cultivated and intensified by man himself when he meditates and contemplates.

The liturgy of religion must not replace the contemplation of religious people. Religion must lead the way to the highly personal act of contemplation, to the vision of the same, real Christ the rugged, untutored Apostles saw and were captivated by.

Why do so many men excuse themselves from the practice of religion? Do they not find it emasculated? Like a party under indiscreet womanly direction where one cannot settle down into a decent manly discussion?

Allow men a *manly devotion* and they will live the liturgical life.

This emphasis on the interior devotion, on "living" ("and this is eternal life, that you may know God, and Jesus Christ whom he has sent"), happens to be the emphasis of Pope Pius XII's *Mediator Dei,* not the opposite—which is the general false impression engendered by quoting Pius out of context. The Pope said: ". . . the most pressing duty of Christians is to live the liturgical life. . . ." So many have put stress on *liturgical*. But the context shows it to be on *live*.

The harmonious environment and salutary discipline created by religion are indispensable for the richest and most fruitful type of mystical experience.

The Christian mystic—that is to say, any man who lives a deep spiritual life—grows up in the Christian society, in the liturgical life of the Church. As Evelyn Underhill says, when he cuts himself away from this source, and depends solely on direct inspiration, "he becomes like a poet who refuses to be controlled by the laws of prosody, which seem to limit but really strengthen and beautify his work."*

Union with, and submission to, the Church, to the family life of God—an attitude of self-giving surrender: this is the best preparation for that total self-naughting of the man involved in union with God; that utter doing away with possessiveness—the I, the Me, and the Mine—until man's spirit becomes one mind and one love with the divine mind and love.

* *Mysticism* (New York: E. P. Dutton, 1957).

Liturgical prayer, that is, the public, solemn, official prayer of the Church, was the subject of the past chapter. Our present concern is with the private prayer of the individual called by God into a unique, personal, solitary communion.

This personal communion is designated above, in the chapter head, as *mental* prayer. The designation is not meant to imply an absence of mental activity in liturgical prayer. The distinction lies rather in the fact that while private prayer is predominantly an activity of the intellect, liturgy is, above all, a system of actions, of which prayer constitutes only one element.

In personal prayer the individual faces God. It is in virtue of this personal encounter that we rise to the dignity of being individual selves. This extremely precious and God-given individuality finds its expression in personal prayer, which is a dialogue between the *one* individual and God.

Men do not stand before God in droves, but each one stands before Him as if he were the only one in the whole world. "On Mt. Carmel, God alone and I." The even more perfect formulation of this relationship is contained in that telling sentence of the Apocalypse (2:7): "He that hath an ear, let him hear what the Spirit saith to the churches, to him that overcometh, I will give the hidden manna and will give him a white counter, and in the counter a new name written, which no man knoweth, but he that receiveth it."

The clearest and most balanced expression of the relationship of public and private prayer that I have ever seen is found in the final pages of Romano Guardini's *Prayer in Practice*. Here the renowned author describes the interdependence of liturgical and personal prayer. Each of these, he says, springs from its own source; yet they act together to form the whole of the Christian life.

Guardini begins by speaking of the liturgy, the divine service of God instituted by Christ, which is perpetually reenacted by the Church. This is essentially the worship of the Church as a whole, but in order to be true worship, it must be expressed by the individuals who compose the Church. Into this corporate worship of the Church the individual merges his own personal religious life, but this life must first exist independently if his participation is to be more than merely superficial. The service of the Church cannot be performed except by the priest and congregation worshiping as individuals. The liturgy, then, gives form to the worship of the Church, but it must find expression through the inner life of each individual. If this inner life is not characterized by an awareness of God, speaking to Him in prayer and listening to His voice, it cannot provide a living channel through which the liturgical service may flow.

If the liturgy cannot have life without the individual, neither may the individual separate himself from the prayer of the Church. This truth is based not only on the individual's need for the faith and intercessory power of the Church. It is evident from the peculiar weakness which is difficult to avoid in private prayer. The very distinguishing characteristics of private prayer—aloneness, interior experience, freedom of development and original expression—may spell danger. The protection against this lies in informing this subjective element of prayer with what is objective and universal. The liturgy not only instructs the worshiper in the form of divine service, but it also provides its content, the norms of a devotion that is genuine, wholesome, and true. At this point the author makes a fine distinction between "personal" and merely "subjective" prayer. Personal prayer has its roots in the dignity of the human person as such. It arises from the center of the soul in touch with its Creator and Redeemer. Prayer becomes subjective when the individual tends to seek himself, replacing revealed truth with his own doubtful impressions and sentiments of religion. In order to strengthen and purify his interior life, the believer must expose it continually to the discipline of the liturgy by regularly taking part in its grandeur and well-ordered ritual. Otherwise, his private prayer may deteriorate into something sentimental, bizarre, or even unhealthy.

Guardini mentions another form of prayer which, along with private prayer, runs similar risks. This is popular devotion, which finds its place and value only where the liturgical life is properly understood and appreciated. Without such a safeguard, popular devotion is apt to deteriorate, to become unintelligent, fantastic, sentimental, and out of proportion. When religious impulse is allowed to rule unchecked, it attenuates the contents of faith, replacing them with meaningless repetition and artificial and sentimental feeling.

With all these justifiable precautions, the author warns us not to go to extremes. It is a great mistake to look down with contempt on all popular devotion or to think of these various forms of prayer as being in any way mutually exclusive. It is equally wrong to disregard personal prayer or to consider it as infringing upon the domain of the liturgy. These attitudes of mind are not only false but dangerous. Guardini concludes his thought with a lovely simile. Popular devotion is to the life of religion what the bond with family, people, home and country, is to the natural life. To deny the rightful place of popular devotion and personal prayer is to declare one's loyalty only to the world and to humanity as a whole; it is to renounce one's need for a people, for a homeland.

Human life was meant to be a response to God's love. It came to be, in fact, a perfect, adequate response in the one single instance of the life of Christ, God incarnate. The Church is the Mystical Body of Christ. It prolongs the Incarnation. It perpetuates the perfect response of Christ. The liturgy is the expression of this worshipful response of the whole Christ. The liturgy provides, then, always, and in every place, the general, objective pattern of prayer. It is within this inspired framework that every man learns to respond as an individual, unique, distinct, unrepeatable.

The full efficacy of liturgical prayer depends upon how well the individual worshiper has learned to respond individually; how thoroughly he has put on the mind of Christ, to what extent he has been "divinized." That is why it is a mistake to say that whenever and however a man offers Mass he is engaging in the highest form of charity. This is true only of Christ. It is true of the rest of us only to the extent that we can say: "I live now, not I, but Christ lives within me."

This progressive transformation into Christ happens to be the indispensable business of mental prayer. It must begin by entering into the right relationship with Christ. He has become our brother, He is the firstborn, we are His brethren, says St. Paul. He is the Master, we are the disciples. He is the One who leads us, who knows the way, who is the example. We are the ones who must follow Him. "I am the way, the truth, and the life. No man cometh unto the Father, but by me" (Jn 14:6). He is the one who reveals the living manifestation of the Father. We behold His face, and "he that seeth me seeth the Father also" (Jn 14:9).

Praying to Christ means entering into this relationship, understanding it, enacting it, dwelling in the relationship which He has established. In this prayer the worshiper implores the Lord to reveal Himself, he quietly dwells in the presence of Christ, adheres to Him with simple, loving attention, ponders over His life and His words, tries to enter into His truth. He seeks *instruction, transformation,* and *conformity.*

When we were baptized, we were supernaturally endowed and adequately equipped to become instructed, transformed, and conformed, in the Christ-life, to become progressively identified with the divine nature we came to share through grace. The powers of this new supernatural organism are faith, hope, and charity.

How are these powers exercised, so that the Christ-life grows and develops in us, so that we are led gradually, graciously, to the pinnacle of all human achievements, union with God? The theological virtues are thrown into action, primarily, by prayer. They become functional through prayer.

Our Lord said: "I no longer call you servants but friends." Christ's expression of this unspeakably wonderful friendship takes place predominantly in prayer wherein He reveals Himself as He promised: "If you love me . . . I will reveal myself to you." And with infinite zeal He desires to do so. We, on our part, respond to this friendship by prayer, wherein we share with Christ the secrets of the Godhead: "Whatsoever things I have ever heard my Father say to me in the bosom of the Godhead I have shared with you."

So it is in prayer that we come to know God as He is in Himself; still, of course, "as through a misty glass." It is through prayer that we come to know Him, no longer by hearsay, but by experience.

Christ came to establish friendship with God. Friendship requires sustained contact. Prayer is man's chief source of contact with God. Aristotle said that it is of the nature of friends to spend as much time as possible delighting in one another's company. And that is one big reason why we pray.

Another reason is that deep in the heart of man is the longing, fitfully glimpsed and but half realized, to gather up —recollect—his manifold, disparate strivings into a unified, intense pursuit of one all-embracing objective worthy of the sweat and labor and devotion of the human heart. But the trivial seems so immediately urgent, the tawdry so ubiquitous, the mundane commands such attention that few men are capable of cultivating a real perspective of value, a unity of design, an intensity of single, concentrated purpose.

A man can achieve this immense human dignity and force by prayer. In a reverent, God-filled upswing of soul he comes as close as his finite nature will allow him to that sublime fusion of all his activities into one glowing point of heat and light. Prayer is, therefore, one of the essentials of our life.

That is why we are commanded by the Word of God in Scripture "to pray without ceasing." It is as if our Lord said: "Do not stop breathing or you will die." The fact is that praying is as necessary for the life of the soul as breathing is for the life of the body. The trouble is we breathe by instinct but we don't pray by instinct. Once we did, or, at least, our first parents did; but they lost the knack of it by committing original sin. Everything depends now upon our regaining it.

And so the author of *De Adhaerendo Deo* writes: "The goal of all perfection is this that the spirit is freed from all carnal inclinations and is lifted up into the spiritual until every word and every volition becomes one continuous prayer."

How can we pray without ceasing? It seems like an impossible sort of command; not for long though, if you think of the common, generic definition of prayer: a raising of the mind and heart to God. This can be done by anyone, anywhere, intermittently, all day long; and in a vague, obscure sort of way, it can be done without intermission. "An obscure sort of way" is something akin to a dog's continued awareness of his master's presence—or, even of his absence which is still an awareness of the master (this is very frequently the way we become contemplative: aridly and obscurely—aware of our Master).

The finest thing to notice about this prayer is that it is a "raising up" not a "withdrawal within." It is God-centered, not man-centered. Prayer thus becomes such an unselfconscious and unpretentious absorption in God, that as St. Anthony, the hermit, said: "He prays best who doesn't even know he's praying."

This ardent, vital passivity flows ineluctably from the fact that prayer is a divine gift. God must first stir us up before we can seek Him. He must take the initiative. It's the Bridegroom's prerogative. His spirit breathes and sighs in us an unceasing "Abba."

The man of prayer, then, knows that his praying is not his own work, his own achievement, that it does not rise up out of his own heart but comes down from above, steams out of the plenitude and power of God. The mysterious impulse which drives him to pray is the revelation of the indwelling God at work in the deepest places of his soul. Christian prayer is, therefore, a spiritual echo: "it is God's voice sounding in the human heart and resounding up to the heaven whence it comes," as A. Stolz remarks.

This does not mean that the gift of prayer is to be passively awaited for and passively received; it is to be consciously and sagaciously sought, cultivated, and practiced. Man must make a colossal effort to introduce prayer into every aspect of his life.

Daily prayer, the enduring sense of His presence, keeps men alive to God. Consequently, because of this constant frame of reference even what is monotonous and momentary becomes momentous. Awareness of God's reality does not eclipse man's view of earthly reality: it heightens it, it enlarges his perspective, and dilates his heart to the dimensions of the universe, even to the compass of Christ's own heart, to the breadth of His universal love. Thus a man of prayer has no scorn, disdain, or even indifference for the world of human things, the world of the flesh, of materiality, of squalor. He loves God's world, God's creatures; and by his love he extends his pure, clean hands into the corrupt and squalid world—and to the extent that he does, he heals and saves the world and restores all things in Christ.

This openness of heart, this alertness to reality empowers a man not only to live but also to die. Not to pray daily means that we are ignoring God, not listening for His word, and not preparing every day for our decisive trials. Thus we are in danger of becoming gradually blind and deaf, indifferent and lazy. In fact, we will lose that capacity to notice the decisive moments when we are at the crossroads of life. A sudden storm will find us without foundation. We will be weak and insecure in that decisive hour when life and death are in the balance, because it will arrive imperceptibly, unannounced. And we will be forced to pay the dreadful price for our refusal to keep alert, active, and responsive to daily prayer. The big decisions of our life are made long before the crucial incidents in the moments in prayer.

Prayer does not exist apart from the ordinary, workaday life of sinful man. It permeates, transforms, and crowns that life. The whole of life is a challenge to prayer. Happy events call for one kind of prayer; sad events, for another. Success and failure, enthusiasm and distress, illness and recovery, birth and death; everything that happens in life must find expression in prayer and determine its nature. We must become sensitive, more inventive. Prayer should not be a daily routine, characterized by the selfsame thoughts and words while life passes on in all its kaleidoscopic diversity.

Things deceive us by being more real than they seem. We overcome this deception by prayer, whereby we grasp the inner core and significance of the things and events of the world which, in turn, lead us on to meditate upon the eternal, timeless reality of God, through whom everything exists.

Life is more than breathing in and breathing out. Life is
—or should be—self-experience and ultimately self-realization.
How much there is in us which we do not realize; indeed,
which seems unrealizable. That is because we are drawn so
readily to the surface, to the periphery; away from the deeps
and center of human life. This leaves one but the shell of a
man: superficial, fragmented, distracted, unrealized. The way
back to the center, to the depths, to maturity, to self-
realization is the way of prayer.

Romano Guardini in his book quoted earlier speaks of the
transfiguring effects of a life governed by prayer. Such a life
will contain moments of illumination when quite ordinary
objects and events will appear suddenly transformed before
our eyes. Shedding the disguise of matter-of-fact existence,
they become freed in our minds in order to reveal themselves
to us as belonging to the realm of mystery. At such times, he
says, we catch glimpses of that hidden plan, which is visibly
projected in the events of human life.

A man of prayer thus becomes acutely aware of and deli-
cately responsive to the miracle of life. A miracle, in its deepest sense, is a "sign" from God—a state of transfiguration in
which the most ordinary object or some commonplace event
suddenly shines in the light of God.

It is out of this basic attitude of soul engendered by prayer
—the idea of the holy, the awe and wonder in face of the
sacred mystery of life—that all the fundamental forms of
prayer flow:

Adoration—the unreserved inclination and self-oblivious
surrender of man to the infinitely live, good, personal God;
the burning but tranquil recognition of the truth, the foundation of all truth, that God is God: unique, alone, and wholly
other, and that man is God's creature. A living response to
this truth in prayer is of greater therapeutic value to man
than any of the psychological discoveries of recent years. It
is, above all, by this adoring response that man maintains his
integrity and wholeness. Adoration is the act in which man's
inner truth continually rises resplendent, in which it is ac-
knowledged and consummated.

If man gets his basic relationship with God right through

adoration, then everything else in his life tends to fall into place. There will be an undeviating "tranquillity of order." And that, says St. Augustine, is the definition of peace.

This form of prayer may be expressed formally, officially, in the words of the liturgist: "*Sanctus, sanctus, sanctus*"; or spontaneously in the words of the little girl overwhelmed by the greatness of God: "Oh Lord, my name is mud."

Thanksgiving—the noblest kind of giving, the refusal to take things for granted; the great-souledness of the liturgist saying in the *Gloria* of the Mass: "We thank Thee, O Lord, for Thy great glory"; and the hilarious delight of the child rollicking in the gifts of God, kissing all the flowers and trees and shouting: "That's a kiss for Jesus."

Reparation—the desire to make up for sin, to repent, restore, atone; *atonement:* the thirst and hunger to be identified with the beloved, to do what He did on the cross for love of God and man.

Petition—openheartedness. It doesn't matter much what we ask for, as long as we let the prayer of petition break through the closed mind and melt the hard heart; as long as we leave ourselves open to the relentless onslaught of God's ennobling love.

These basic forms of prayer are all, of course, interconnected. They are but different aspects of the living relationship of man to God, made possible because God reveals Himself to man and calls him by name into a personal encounter of love.

A man will never gain facility in this generic form of prayer —living always in the presence of God, at home, on the street, at work, at play—unless he sets aside, faithfully, day after day, silent, solitary periods for a very specific, deep, concentrated form of prayer.

This form of prayer is defined by St. Teresa as "a heart to heart conversation with God, our Father who, we know, loves us." Such prayer is not best realized by brilliant ideas, fervent feelings, sweet consolations, or clear images. It is at heart an awareness of God, His reality, closeness, and love, beyond the depths and with an impact ordinarily unattainable by less profound and unconcentrated moments of prayer.

Concentration on any level is not easily come by. That is why this highest form of human concentration demands technique, discipline, regularity, stubbornness, and perhaps, above all, *time*—time to settle down, become composed, restful, collected. One needs, at least, fifteen uninterrupted minutes, gradually prolonged.

Since prayer is, sorry to say, an art, we've got to work long and hard at learning it. We've got to be methodical. So ordinarily a beginner, and sometimes an old-timer, needs to use a method. It must be used judiciously, not slavishly. Otherwise, it will be a crippling, stifling thing rather than a help. And the kind of method one uses must be carefully chosen. It must be suitable. The purpose of a method is similar to the purpose of a scaffolding in erecting a building. As the building goes up the scaffolding is gradually discarded. The thing we are trying to achieve in prayer is access to God, friendship with Him. As this is attained the method is eventually scrapped. It may be resorted to again during distracted or disorganized phases of life. It is a sometime thing; a crutch.

There are many kinds of methods. But there are a few basic factors common to them all.

I. *Preparation*

After resolutely setting aside a definite period of quiet for personal communion with God in mental prayer, it is then necessary to prepare for it; first remotely then proximately.

By *remote* preparation is meant the way we spend the day. We tend to think of prayer as a means toward having a good, holy, happy day. That is certainly true to an extent. But it is true to an even greater extent to put it the other way around. We try to be charitable, prudent, God-conscious all day long in order to pray well when it comes time for that vastly important engagement with no less a person than God. The key word for this remote preparation is *recollection* or Christian inwardness: directing everything in life to God.

By proximate preparation is meant the way we tone up the mind and calm down the passions, etc., immediately prior to the specific periods of prayer. This is ordinarily best done by well-chosen meditative reading; for instance, *The Life of*

Christ, or whatever proves to be most suitable to a particular person at a particular time.

II. *Imagination*

The heart of prayer is the conversation. The average person cannot converse with God instinctively, spontaneously. What we need to do, therefore, is set the stage for this kind of personal communion with God. Most people find that good use of the imagination is the first step toward this.

By becoming *incarnate* God has provided the imaginal background for our prayer. By fixing our imagination on some scene from our Lord's life we begin to pray.

III. *Meditation*

Once we have projected an image of Christ (being scourged, for instance) we commence to reflect on this: Who is this being scourged? Why? What has it got to do with me? This is meditation.

It is important here to note how meditation is just a step toward prayer (we are still setting the stage, creating the atmosphere). It is misleading to call prayer "meditation." It is also disheartening. Many people are frightened off from prayer precisely because they think of it in terms of meditation: a highly rational, logical process of ratiocination. But meditation is only a step—an extremely important one—toward the "heart to heart conversation with God."

IV. *Conversation*

This is the crown and culmination of prayer. It is, basically, a prayer of affection; not especially characterized by emotion or sentiment, but by strong loving acts of the will. If these affections were to be verbalized, they would come out something like this: "My God, I love You." "Lord, keep Your hand upon my head today, lest I offend You." "Let me take good care of You in my neighbor today." These affections are vital. They tend toward action and shape the thinking and behavior of the man of prayer.

Conversation, as used here, is a many-splendored thing. When the devout man has poured forth to God all his heart, his misery and joy, he inwardly pauses with the petition: "Speak, Lord, for Thy servant heareth." And God speaks to the silent and attentive person, He reveals to him His will, answers his questions, resolves his doubts, stills his longing, and soothes his pains.

Conversation may mean a veritable dialogue. It may be an imageless, wordless awareness of God's presence. It may be a poignant, anxious searching or empty waiting for the Lord. It may be a silent, pleasant enjoyment of His company. It certainly should not be a veritable Vesuvius of monologue, a selfish indulgence in the pleasures of loquacity, or misguided sentiment.

If one is graced to begin with this kind of prayer, then he ought to skip the preliminary steps. There would be no need at the moment to resort to reading, imagining, and meditating. St. John of the Cross says that if you find an orange peeled you eat it; you don't try peeling it again.

Here is a simple fundamental principle: anything you can do at prayer to heighten awareness of God makes good prayer.

You learn to pray by praying. A child learns to talk by talking. The first verbal noises a child makes seem meaningless and useless; but if he ceases to make these noises he never learns to talk. So often, especially at the beginning, our prayer seems meaningless and useless, full of dryness and distractions and perhaps sleep; but if we were to give up prayer because of these difficulties, we would never learn to pray.

Distractions are in the mind. One kind of distraction is a consequence of a day ill-spent. If, for instance, a person is committing deliberate venial sins, or is inordinately attached to created pleasures, or even excessively preoccupied with his own work, then he is going to suffer a hangover in the form of distractions in prayer. This kind of distraction he must stand firm against and try to eliminate by a very careful remote preparation.

There is another kind of distraction that crops up in prayer. It is much less pernicious than the former, and more readily managed. After one has made some progress in prayer, he becomes less dependent on the imagination; and so he ceases to use it. Well, this second kind of distraction is simply the imagination coming down off the shelf and getting back into the act. The best way to cope with it is to ignore it. A person can go on praying while in the background this weird and fantastic parade of images concocted by an offended, unused imagination will gradually peter out, if ignored.

Dryness or aridity is also a difficulty met by those who are learning to pray. This is a problem of the will. When one is assailed by aridity his attempts at mental prayer result in disgust and he is strongly tempted to give up then and there. He has no fervor, no sense of God's presence, no recognizable capacity for praying at all.

There are three principal causes of aridity. One is the same sort of condition that causes distraction: a sinful, dissipated, thoughtless habit of living. You can't pass, magically, from godlessness to godliness. The mind is like a sponge and the memory stores up whatever is digested by the mind. We are at every moment—even moments of prayer—very largely what we were; and no one can instantaneously rub clean the slate of his experiences. What was opposed to God cannot suddenly become subject for conversation with Him.

If a person is physically unfit, because of either sickness, fatigue, or mental anxiety, he will, inevitably, be bothered by dryness at prayer.

Sometimes it is God's own way of shaking someone out of lethargy, complacency, and self-satisfaction, or His way of purifying and detaching man, driving him by grace of the "dark nights," where there is no sensible devotion and no creature comfort and no consolation—driving him beyond the creature to the Creator, beyond the gifts to the Giver.

The existence of distractions and aridity in prayer do not impede growth. They may, in fact, be a great means of growth. Half an hour of prayer spent in battling distractions and overcoming sleep may be more soul-sanctifying and world-redeeming than an equal period of brilliant ideas, impressive images, and fine feelings.

Abbot Chapman in his *Spiritual Letters** says that:

Possibly the best kind of prayer is when we are unable to do anything, if then we throw ourselves on God and stay con-

* London: Sheed and Ward Limited, 1954.

tentedly before Him; worried, anxious, tired, listless, but above all, under it all—humbled and abandoned to His will, contented with our own discontent. If we can get ourselves accustomed to this attitude of soul, which is always possible, we have learned how to pray, and we can pray for any length of time—the longer the better—and at any time.

These difficulties may, indeed, be the first sign of progress. Learning to pray is like learning to read. Tyro readers need pictures to attract them, to capture their fancy, appeal to their senses, and urge them on. Beginners in prayer need plenty of images too, for the very same reason. And God, who draws all things, all people, to Himself sweetly, graciously, according to our nature, gives us at first sensible devotion, fervor, clear images and ideas—thus drawing us to Himself.

But just as it would be cruelty on the part of any teacher not to wean the child away from pictures to the words themselves, and thus to deprive the child of the art of reading, of the pleasure of deep knowledge and understanding, so it would be equally cruel of God to go on feeding the man of prayer with baby food; feelings, images, and ideas of God; never weaning him away from the shadow, the reflection, and introducing him to the Word Himself; and thus depriving him of the art of prayer and the substantial joys of wisdom.

The weaning away, the purifying process, the deepening and enlivening of faith, involve necessarily some degree and some phases of darkness on two levels: the "night of the senses" and the "night of the spirit."

The emptying process leading to the fullness of the Christian life, the fullness of prayer life, by which a man becomes a great lover of God and of His whole creation, is brought about not by God alone but by the cooperative ascetic efforts of the creature. Without a real, sustained effort of the creature to mortify sense, to overcome evil tendencies, no true advance in prayer can be made. This effort must include interior mortification which aims at conquering self-love, checking unruly thoughts and affections, weaning the desires from all that is not God. If this is done as the soul strives for divine union, God will reveal Himself, manifest His presence, and perhaps grant the person of prayer an experiential awareness of this union.

The progression of prayer is characterized by increased *simplicity*. One's relationship with God and the conversation become more and more ruled by one thing: love. And so prayer becomes progressively: loving attention to God, abiding in His presence, a simple awareness of God through the mist and the haze as well as in the light. And all the time there are fewer human ways and modes of operation to support (or hinder) this sacred art of communion.

This simple and more advanced form of prayer is dominated by the activity of the Holy Spirit through the actuation of the theological virtues and the gifts, especially wisdom. This is contemplative prayer. It is a very normal and very desirable form of prayer within the reach of all, to be desired by all. Under the dominating action of the Holy Spirit a man becomes less imaginative, aggressive, talkative, more silent, docile, receptive, responsive, and passive (in the sense of "suffering the transforming action of God").

There are five fundamental stages in contemplation: recollection, quiet, union, espousals, and mystical marriage. The first three belong to conforming union, the other two to transforming union. These are not strict categorical divisions but general, loose, overlapping, rhythmic movements of spiritual growth following a faithful, well-disciplined, generous period of life wherein one engages in more or less discursive meditation.

It is not good to be unduly, if at all, concerned about one's own stage of prayer. All one needs to know is when prayer is changing from meditation to contemplation so as to adjust properly and not spoil things by turmoil, fear, ignorance, kicking against the goad, or giving up.

There are signs of this transition which can be recognized with the help of a director:

1. Inability to meditate—that is, to use reason and imagination in the things of God. God is communicating Himself no longer by way of sense. He is transforming the strength of the senses to the spirit.

2. There is no consolation from God but neither is there

from any creature. Imagination is restless. But there is no desire to fix the senses on the world.

3. The memory is centered obscurely but lovingly on God. There is a certain deep-seated pleasure in being alone with God. There this loving, vague, general knowledge or quiet peace of the faculties alternates with painful aridity and distraction, until it finally becomes habitual.

If these three conditions prevail simultaneously, then a man should know that God is introducing him to contemplation, to a deeper, richer form of prayer, less dependent on the senses. He should not, then, on his part, make frantic efforts to meditate, but remain calm and tranquil, but spiritually alive to God.

To be a contemplative, therefore, is to follow out perfectly the First Commandment, and to imitate Christ in His most characteristic activity. Contemplation is not a spiritual luxury, something off the main line of sanctity. It is the simplest, most mature, most solid Christianity. To become like Christ is to become more and more contemplative. There is no other way. The religion of Christianity is, at its depths, a mystical life. A Christian who lives this life deeply is living the mystical life, is, to a degree, a mystic: one who knows God by experience, by an intuition born of love. This love is ignited in prayer.

No man comprehends God in this world or out of it. No man escapes God. No one can live in this world unmoved by God. In the present dispensation, every man's position before God remains unfixed. If a man's union with God is not being progressively intensified, then he is retrogressing from his first love. Life is essentially bound up with movement; it is an approach toward a goal. A man is stable—not static—to the extent that he makes a relentless effort to attain an object beyond his reach—"a pressing toward the mark," as St. Paul calls it.

The consistent growth of one's spiritual life is absolutely necessary. If one ceases to advance toward God, he is moving away from the source and end of his life. If he stands still, he stagnates. If he accepts the *status quo*, his present achievement, as ultimate, he disintegrates and undoes all that was previously well done.

When you know what a man is made *of* and *for*, you can expect a certain kind of behavior and growth, and you will know how to measure his growth in terms of his goal and endowments.

The last end of the human being is union with God. And it is charity that unites him to God—"Whoever abides in charity abides in God, and God in him." The end, which is charity, admits of no measure. But the end need not, in fact cannot, be achieved immediately. It may be achieved one way or another. And there are degrees of love. To love God at all is already, in some sense, to possess Him. "The lowest degree of divine love is to love nothing more than God, nothing contrary to God, nothing as much as God. He who does not reach this degree of Christian perfection in no way accomplishes the precept" (Cajetan). The precept referred to is the command "To be perfect . . . to love God with the whole mind and whole heart." The highest possible degree of union with God is that enjoyed in the Beatific Vision; the highest possible in this life is that of mystical experience, which is enjoyed in the prayer of contemplation. When Cajetan speaks of the degree of perfection compatible with the present life, he says it demands: ". . . the exclusion of everything repugnant to the movement of love toward God. This is realized when a man excludes from his affection not only everything incompatible with the existence of charity, such as mortal sin, but also everything that prevents the affection of the soul being directed wholly on God."

Contemplation, which is an experiential, loving, and ineffable knowledge of God, is the supreme means of attaining the perfection of charity. "For how shall a man attain to the perfection of charity, if he does not keep himself habitually in the presence of God, and has not the attention of his whole soul fixed on Him and primarily on Jesus Crucified in such a way as to pass through the wounds of His humanity into the intimacy of the divinity?"

The goal of supernatural life, then, for every baptized person is a loving experiential knowledge of God, intimate union accomplished through sanctifying grace—the same grace that all of us possess—the theological virtues, and the gifts of the Holy Spirit.

Love, intimate love, is the heart of mysticism.

Mystical contemplation, in its highest degree, is thus the term or goal of the Christian life. Although it is a free gift of God, St. John of the Cross assures us that it will usually be obtained by those who, progressing in perfection, dispose themselves for it.

After all, will not our Lord keep His promises? "He that loves me shall be loved by my Father: and I will love him and manifest myself to him. . . . My Father will love him and we will come to him and make our abode with him" (Jn 21:23). And this infused knowledge and love by which God reveals Himself is essentially the same beatitude the blessed enjoy in heaven. "For this is eternal life: that they may know thee, the only true God, and Jesus Christ whom thou hast sent" (Jn 17:3).

No wonder this intimate knowledge of the Holy Trinity and of Christ, the Word Incarnate, opens up infinite depths of joy and peace to the contemplative Christian. "These things I have spoken to you that my joy may be in you, and your joy may be filled. . . . Peace I leave with you, my peace I give you. Not as the world gives do I give unto you . . ." (Jn 14:27). The joy of the contemplative is consummated in perfect union: "The glory which thou hast given me I have given them; that they may be one as we also are one: I in them and thou in me, that they may be made perfect in one" (Jn 17:22, 23).

If a man would use with maximal effort his supernatural equipment "stirring up the grace that is within him," he would come in a short time to know God by experience, which is contemplation. Contemplation is the result of a normal full development of supernatural life. Contemplation may not and need not always be felt, but it is present when there is healthy spiritual growth. Where there is no contemplation, there is stunted growth, for contemplation is nothing more than the actuation and gradual development of the theological virtues and the gifts, particularly wisdom.

Is a man adequately equipped to reach these normal but towering objectives of the spiritual life? Even a meager consciousness of our supernatural organism ought to convince us of the affirmative answer to this question. The resplendent, ineffable life of God unfolds within the soul of every baptized person. Grace is the cause of that inner life.

It is by faith and the sacraments that a man is first confronted by God, introduced into the living Mystical Body of Christ, endowed with power from on high. At that first contact with God, a man is imbued with perfections of an immeasurably higher order than he could hope to achieve by a lifetime of moral effort. By grace man partakes of the intimate life of the Godhead, not because he has rendered service to the Deity, but because he is the object of divine Love who bestows upon man an incomparable free gift to which he has no right. God not only takes the initiative in the spiritual life of men, but He sustains and dominates the whole movement of the human being to the divine Being.

Man is equipped by nature with a rational soul comprising the faculties of intellect and will. He achieves natural perfection by employing these powers upon their proper objects in the business of knowing and loving. By the infusion of grace a whole new supernatural world is opened up. The soul is divinized in its essence through a participation in the divine nature, and the faculties are simultaneously elevated by the virtues and gifts. The performance of these supernatural powers or "habits" perfect the grace-endowed soul, as knowing and loving perfect it on the plane of nature.

These virtues and gifts make up the faculties of man's new supernatural being. By means of them he can learn to inhale and exhale in a manner that is inexpressibly wonderful because it is divine. For, as Thomas Merton put it: "Then he shall be constantly breathing with the very breath of God, that is to say, he shall receive into his soul the 'spiration' of the Holy Spirit, and he shall mystically breathe this divine Spirit of love back into God. . . ." Human intimacy with God is founded upon the sublime mystery of the indwelling of the Blessed Trinity in the soul.

"Come then, thou soul, most beautiful of all creatures, that so greatly desires to know the place where thy Beloved is in order to seek Him and be united with Him; now thou art told that thou thyself art the lodging wherein He dwells, and the closet and hiding place wherein He is hidden. Thus it is a matter of great contentment and joy for thee to see that all thy good and thy hope are so near thee as to be within thee, or to speak more exactly, so near that thou canst not be without them. . . . What more desirest thou, O soul, and what more seekest thou without thyself, since within thyself thou hast thy riches, thy delights, thy satisfaction, thy fulness, and thy kingdom, which is thy Beloved, whom thy soul desires and seeks? Rejoice and be glad in thy inward recollection with Him, since thou hast Him so near" (St. John of the Cross, *Spiritual Canticle*).

Catechism awareness of what happens at baptism is not enough. It is necessary to consider the gifts and promises of God in their integral beauty. To be born again to the life of children of God does not mean only to be converted to the state of grace, but to be completely despoiled of the false self, to renounce creatures completely, and to adhere perfectly to the will of God.

Contemplation will not be given to those who willfully remain at a distance from God, who confine their interior life to a few routine exercises of piety and a few external acts of worship and service performed as a matter of duty.

Grace makes a man, at least potentially, like Christ. At baptism one becomes Christ, and so in a way prolongs His Incarnation in the world. But he has got to become Christ in reality, growing up in Him, putting on His mind, conforming to Him, achieving the fullness of His stature. What is needed is that our merely human activities should become imbued with the waters of eternal life flowing from the fountain, planted by God within the soul; or to speak more strictly in the words of Dom Aelred Graham: "That the soul with its twin faculties of intellect and will—the *mens* of the theologians, . . . the focal point of all personal union with God—being divinized by the infusion of grace, should dominate the whole man, . . . shedding the light of heaven upon each of his actions."[*] This is what it means to really become Christ. It does not happen overnight. It involves growth—a long arduous process of maturing.

The best way to grow is to act like Christ—a tall order. But our supernatural organism makes us tall men, Godlike men. So we can act like Christ. Faith, hope, and charity enable us to do so.

Faith empowers a man to know God in the manner that Christ knows him. By faith he envisions his final goal; he sees all against the background of eternity, thanks to the divine perspective of reality he shares with Christ.

Hope is a push Godward. So awed by the dark vision of God engendered by faith, so overcome by the transcendence of the mighty and majestic God, a man could not even begin to aspire to union with Infinite Goodness unless he were moved and goaded on to bold and daring aspirations by the virtue of hope.

[*] Dom Aelred Graham, *The Love of God* (New York: Doubleday [Image Books], 1959), p. 92.

Charity is union with God. It is to love God in the manner that Christ loves His Father. It unites and transforms the human person into Christ.

Of all the powers possessed by a grace-endowed soul, charity is the greatest, being, as it is, the bond of all the others and their crown. In all creation, there is nothing superior to the supernatural love of God, except the light of glory possessed by saints in heaven.

This charity, as Dom Aelred says, is not just a succession of good deeds, but "a vital tendency" implanted in the very depths of the spirit by which the spirit moves, "in the light of faith," upward and outward—toward God in longing and toward the neighbor in good will and enlightened activity.†

It is by the activity of the dynamic theological virtues that men achieve spiritual growth—the progressive enlightenment of the mind and enlargement of the heart. This kind of development depends most of all upon charity.

God is life (cf. Jn 14:6). He is also love (cf. Jn 4:16). As the supernatural life of man is a sharing in the divine life, so charity is a sharing in the infinite love of God. To be endowed with supernatural life is to possess supernatural love—"the charity of God is poured forth in our hearts by the Holy Spirit who has been given to us" (Rom 5:5). As physical life is inevitably expressed in movement, so spiritual life is expressed in love; and life is strong to the degree that love is ardent. Life is given to us in grace, and grace, if we are responsive and generous, will unite us more and more intimately to God in love. And although charity is a free gift of God, we are ourselves in a very large measure responsible for the degree and intensity of our love, for the increase of charity is a reward merited by our correspondence with grace.

If there is no growth of supernatural life it means there is no love. Lifelessness is lovelessness. Whatever impedes or hampers love weakens life. Whatever enkindles love engenders life.

It is not enough to know how magnificently God has en-

† *Op. cit.*, p. 98.

riched the human person with supernatural life, granted him a Godlike mode of existence. One must inquire how this seed of glory maintains and develops its rather precarious existence here below, pending the attainment of full fruition and unending quiescence in the light of the Beatific Vision. Generally speaking, there are two positive ways: through the instrumentality of the sacraments and by the acts of the virtues themselves.

The sacraments are the divinely chosen channels of grace. They are charged with the saving, healing, ennobling power of Christ's Passion, and so the Fathers of the Church have figuratively described them as so many rivers of grace flowing from Christ's side on Calvary.

God has mercifully chosen to draw man to Himself according to his nature—taking him as He finds him. He finds him more prone to material things than to spiritual things and so without doing violence to his weak nature He graciously woos and entices and draws him to Himself by material things, corporeal and sensible signs; but signs which have the marvelous power of effecting what they signify.

It is through the sacramental system, the liturgy—"primary and indispensable source of the true Christian spirit" and of spiritual growth—that Christians not only give glory to God but share His glory as they grow up in Christ.

The Christ-life of the Mystical Body is functional, operating through the organism of the Sacraments, which impart, protect, develop, and fulfill the Divine Indwelling.

In Holy Orders, the visible Priesthood of Christ is preserved until the end of time, when the fullness of the Mystical Body is consummated. By it chosen men are anointed by the Holy Spirit to be progenitors and preservers of the Christ-life, and so we call them Father.

In Matrimony, the force of nuptial love is incorporated into the redemptive, sacrificial love of Jesus for His Mystical Body, and spouses become the ministers of Christ, one to the other, for the furtherance of that work which secures the extension of the Mystical Body.

Baptism is the sacrament of the second birth, establishing the divine life in the soul, and incorporating the recipient as a member of Christ's Mystical Body.

The Eucharist is the Sacrament whereby the Mystical Body sacrifices itself in union with Christ's sacrifice, and receives therefrom the fruit of the Sacrifice for its sustenance and the development of its perfection.

The sacrament of Confirmation exists to confer upon Christians a share in Christ's priestly power for imparting the means of grace to others, especially in Christian education (parents in the home, Sisters in the school, imparting Christian knowledge to their charges), and in the works of Catholic Action, bringing into society Christian principles.

In Penance and Extreme Unction, the Mystical Body has the means of repairing and restoring the Christ-life to its sinful members, and of repairing the losses it sustains from sin.*

And there is above all the great central action of the Church's whole liturgical life, the Mass, in which Christ lives on in the world and in time and by which He draws all things to Himself.

It is in the Mass that we are united to Christ from whom all graces of contemplation flow. Our Lord is, in fact, the very embodiment of contemplation—a human nature united in one Person with the infinite truth and splendor of God. We become liturgists and contemplatives at the same time as we grow in the participation of Christ's divine Sonship; and that participation is granted to us eminently in the Mass.

In the Eucharist Jesus gives us Himself, "the way, the truth, and the life." And so the Blessed Sacrament is not a sign of contemplation; it contains Him who is the beginning and end of all contemplation. Should not, then, the grace of Holy Communion be one of the most normal ways by which normal people come to enjoy contemplation?

The purpose of mental prayer is to activate and exercise the theological virtues of faith, hope, and love so that by their growth and development we can achieve the goal of human life: union with God.

It is one thing to make isolated acts of faith and love; quite another to acquire the habit of making these acts of faith

* From *The Sacramental Way*, ed. Mary Perkins, Copyright 1948, Sheed and Ward, Inc., New York, p. 8. This quotation is from a paper by Rev. Benedict Ehmann.

and love. This is the function of prayer. Faith becomes
functional in prayer and with repetition it becomes habitual
—we can live by faith. Prayer is an expression of faith, a personal, live faith in a living God. What happens when we begin to advance in prayer?—Information becomes conviction;
the outline of Catholic Faith becomes an experience; objective truth becomes a subjective experience. Prayer is theology
lived. The process of becoming a saint is the process of falling
in love. In mental prayer truth becomes excitingly interesting; God reveals Himself. Remember what our Lord said
about our being His friends and no longer just servants?
Why? Because He shares His secrets with us. The saints are
not sterilized beings devoid of feeling and interests. They
are torches aglow with the fire of God's love lighted in prayer.
In prayer, Christ becomes progressively fascinating. We are
haunted by His beauty ever ancient, ever new.

Because we have come to know Him in prayer we fall in
love with Him. It is in the heart-to-heart conversation of mental prayer that love is expressed over and over again, and
thus flamed into intensity. We gradually live by love, and
hence achieve dynamic spiritual growth. That is why St.
Alphonsus, St. Teresa, and Pius XII spoke so unequivocally:

It is morally impossible for him who neglects meditation
to live without sin.

He who neglects mental prayer needs not a devil to carry
him to hell, but he brings himself there with his own hands.
[So not a superfluous nicety, but a basic necessity.]

It must be stated without reservation that no other means
has the unique efficacy of meditation, and that as a consequence, its daily practice can in no wise be substituted for.

The other indispensable means of spiritual growth is a reasonable organic, lifelong program of self-denial. Even for
the bare subsistence of grace and charity asceticism or self-
discipline of some sort is necessary. For growth and development it is absolutely imperative, since detachment from the
things of the world is a condition *sine qua non* of advance-
ment in the love of God. "Love not the things in the world.

If any man love the world, the charity of the Father is not in him" (1 Jn 11:15).

Contemplation will be denied to a man insofar as he belongs to the world. He belongs to the world who allows the world to diminish and divide his love of God. To this extent the world becomes a rival of God. He who divides his affection is not ready—because not empty and receptive—to receive the Holy Spirit who is the love of God. As St. John of the Cross says: "Two contraries cannot coexist at the same time in the same subject."

Only by progressively, sometimes ruthlessly, ridding himself of inordinate love of creatures can a man be filled with love of God. This is true not because creatures are not good; they are very good. It is true only because every man has an uncanny habit of attaching himself to creatures and consuming his energy in a purely natural enjoyment of them. And if a man is deliberately attached to a single thing that is not God, even a trifle, he cannot be attached to God; there will be little progress in perfection, and a very slender sort of spiritual growth.

St. Francis de Sales explains this quite clearly. Since we are finite beings, he says, our capacity for love is limited; hence before our hearts can contain a greater love of God they must be further drained of attachments to creatures.

Our Lord is even clearer: "No man can serve two masters; for either he will hate the one and love the other or else he will stand by the one and despise the other. You cannot serve God and mammon."

There is, then, a twofold movement in the Christian life: one toward God, one away from creatures. It might be better to refer to them as two phases of one movement of the person to God. The one—movement toward God—is positive and it is accomplished by the development of grace, charity, and the gifts. The other, away from creatures, is negative; it is a purification, a process of detachment carried on by mortification and renunciation.

The love of God, the positive factor, being the end, is first in intention, motivating, determining, and guiding every step along the way. But since divine love can only enter into a heart that is stripped bare of all *selfish* affection for creatures, then the work of purification is first in practice.

Both factors are always involved in the life of man with God. One does not wake up one day to the spiritual life and decide to be positive or negative about it, bright or dull, gay or lugubrious. One must take brisk, daring, joyous steps toward God; and at the same time stride deliberately, painstakingly into the world. So there are positive and negative, bright and dark aspects that color the spiritual life of every human being.

If a person thinks a great deal about the effects of God's love in himself, he is going to come out of his meditation walking like a giant, singing like a Julie Andrews, bursting like spring; for he will be engaged by ideas that not only provoke thought but quicken the spirit; astounding, elevating ideas like: a man's supernatural organism, his unspeakably wonderful endowment, his divine equipment, his capacity to know and love God and to share His divine nature, to become an intimate member of the family of God. A man cannot be keenly aware of his exalted, noble condition without being impressed, enthused, and amazed.

If, on the other hand, a person thinks predominantly of the demands of God's love, he is likely to come away from his study a bit overwhelmed. He will be tormented with thoughts like: God is infinitely and supremely good, the only object worthy of all my love. He is a jealous lover, brooking no compromise, no cheap bargaining. And that means an irrevocable commitment, absolute surrender, total dedication. And the trouble is that it cannot be done with one bold reckless gesture, performed once and for all, and then pleasured in. No, it has got to be made and renewed and sustained until death. God's love is devastating, a fire consuming all that natural life a chap would like to hang on to, the few harmless attachments to creatures, the persistent hankering for things of earth. What this means is a ruthless rooting up out of the heart things he has grown too fond of; clearing the road of all that does not facilitate and quicken his steps toward God. And this means discipline, self-abnegation. A man might be just a bit bogged down by the awful burden of such devouring love.

But this negating, and therefore negative aspect, has got to be faced manfully and serenely. This serenity can be achieved ordinarily by turning the other side of the coin, and being recharged by the dynamic, positive factors of the spiritual life: just remembering who started this whole business, and how He will bring it to an end that is happy, joyous, delightful beyond the reach of human dreams, and how in the meantime it is His strength and love and life that sustains us.

It is evident from all that has been said thus far that without steady, consistent progress in perfection there can be no personal fulfillment. Neither can there be a worthwhile contribution to society and a leavening of the mass of humanity.

Nemo dat quod non habet—"No one gives what he doesn't have." Christianity is the fire that Christ came to light in men's hearts and spread through the world. If a man is not aflame with this fire he will not radiate. If an organization is interested in nothing more than a routine, minimum Christianity, how inane the claim of its members that they are engaged in Catholic Action.

Maturity, in the natural plane, is necessary before a man can render appreciable service to others. While immature he must concentrate on his own development. Now, perfection is the maturity of the supernatural life; and it is only as men approximate it that they wield those supernatural powers and energies necessary for reestablishing the kingdom of Christ at the crossroads of the world.

One perfect Christian glorifies God more than thousands of imperfect chosen people. A single act of love on the part of a perfect soul is more pleasing to God than the sum total of all the incomplete acts of love proffered by those who are not perfect. According to St. John of the Cross: "An instant of pure love is more precious in the eyes of God and the soul and more profitable to the Church than all other good works together, though it seems as though nothing were done."

But remember: he said pure love; and before one can do very much of that kind of loving he has got to go through the dark, purifying nights of contemplation. It is just such intrepid warriors and lovers the world needs to withstand Satan. That is why one day the devil appeared to St. John Vianney and confessed openly: "If there were four more men like you in the world I, Satan, would be finished; and my evil forces in the world overcome."

We need perfect Christians, perfect priests, perfect religious, perfect parents, students, officials, workers, employers. If anyone wishes to contribute something valuable to the world, the Church, his country, mankind, he must start with himself by subsuming everything else within the great-souled, absorbing pursuit of transforming union with God.

Accordingly, even the apostle's first concern must be not to enlarge his field of activity but to deepen his interior life. "He that abides in me, the same shall bear much fruit. . . . Seek ye first the kingdom of God."

This is so very true that one good hermit in the desert can change the world, while pretentious organizations, comprising vast numbers of Christians, performing multifarious activities, fail to accomplish anything.

Actually, there is a heavy supply of failure for which to account. Why has paganism won control of the greater part of the world? How has Communism flourished for so long? Why has Christianity had such a meager, paltry impact upon our contemporary society? Christianity has not failed. But in itself it is an abstract thing; and as such it is quite helpless and useless. As G. K. Chesterton put it: "Christianity has not been tried and found wanting; it has been found difficult and left untried." Untried. There's the rub. It has got to take root and come alive and grow in individual lives—in homes, offices, schools, shops, courts, and so on.

If Christian forces have not yet permeated and shaped our institutions, it is primarily because of the stunted spiritual growth of individuals. The seeds of spiritual greatness are planted in every Christian at baptism. But seeds must grow and develop before there can be a harvest. There are thousands of Christians walking about the face of the earth bearing in their bodies the infinite God of whom they know practically nothing.

The seeds of sanctity and contemplation have been sown there by God, but they lie dormant. They do not germinate. In other words: sanctifying grace occupies the substance of their souls, but it is never stirred up and sent flowing out to inflame and irrigate and take possession of the intellect and will. God does not manifest Himself to these souls because they do not really love Him.

They are men divided between God and the world. God rules over them substantially, but their thoughts and desires do not belong to Him. They belong to the world and to external things. Consequently, the Spirit of Truth cannot be received "because they see him not, nor do they know him."

Precisely because of the stunted growth of the individual there is a lack of inner force in those agencies that have for their purpose the promotion of Christ's principles and His way of life. And this is so despite the obvious external strength of these agencies—their brave speeches, impressive programs, and crowded conventions. It is even a mistake, as the Vicar of Christ tells us, to judge the vitality of a parish by the number of communicants.

We have great organizations that do not spread Christian influence because they lack interior force and vitality. Many groups use up their energies in bridge, bowling, and bazaars. They may have no spiritual significance at all. If not, they only reproduce secular societies, wield only secular influence. Organizations that promote successful dances or athletic teams, and are slightly, if at all, concerned with the Christ-life of the members, or with the mission of spreading the life of Christ, are a sheer waste of time.

This strong emphasis on inner growth does not mean that a Christian ought to care for his own soul and let the world go hang. Neither does it mean that a man must be a saint before he can be an apostle. On the contrary, a Christian must grow more and more concerned with the world. He must also act as an apostle intensely and untiringly not after he has reached spiritual maturity, but while he is maturing; just so long as his output is not beyond the strength of his growth. The primacy of the interior life is one of order more than of time.

Activity without contemplation is blind. But activity that is not feverish is, or should be, an aid to contemplation. Activity can be purifying and sanctifying. Inherent in the daily lives of extremely busy people and in the apostolate itself is a wide variety of elements that can raise the mind and heart to God, that can mortify and humiliate as well as inspire, and thus provide a ready-made program of asceticism that will ultimately lead clear-seeing, strong-willed men and women to the pinnacle of all human achievements, namely: spiritual matrimony with God.

Charity, a virtue hidden in the soul, becomes apparent to the world in action. By their fruits you shall know them. Our Lord gives us the right to make external activity a test of the genuineness of our love of God. There is nothing in the world more divine, declares the Pseudo-Denis, than to become a cooperator with God in the salvation of souls.

The important thing to remember is that all human activity must be motivated and crowned with love. The apostle, whether he be priest, religious, or layman, must have a reason for everything he does, and that reason must be Christ.

Cardinal Lavigerie, a famous missionary bishop, spoke terrifying words to his priests: "You must be fully convinced of this, for an apostle there is no middle way between complete holiness, at least in desire, sought after with fidelity and courage, and absolute perversion."

Spiritual growth presupposes roots. We are children of our age, and therefore open to all the influences of our time. If these influences are the only motivating factors of our lives, then we are uprooted and can hardly have life at all. If we do not select and/or reject these influences against a background of nature, origins, ends, and the common, universal experiences of mankind, we weaken and loosen our roots and become like reeds shaken in the wind.

That seems to be the state of mind that characterizes man today. Père Teilhard de Chardin analyzes the condition in this way: "Mankind, taken as a whole, is actually in the process of undergoing, in its own way, a kind of crisis of puberty." Our age, in other words, has all the efflorescent qualities of an eager adolescent who sees all things in the light of his own limited experience.

If we are to mature, we need first of all to reestablish our roots in the Spirit. "Over its (the earth's) waters, brooded the Spirit of God," and by its power emerged heaven and earth. This is the beginning, the source of all things, a creative, life-producing Spirit. "From the clay of the ground, the Lord God formed man, breathed into his nostrils the breath of life, and made man a living soul." This Spirit is the principle of all cosmic and biological life, the source of all existence. "He has but to turn his thought toward men, reclaiming the spirit he once breathed into them, and all life would fail everywhere; mankind would return to its dust" (Jb 34:14–15).

There is, in fact, a certain failure or diminution of life and a pull toward dust when man forgets his spiritual origin and nature and acts out of context. He can remain profoundly and magnificently alive only by cultivating an awareness of his divine origins: the roots of his life are in other worlds. With his roots in the Spirit, he will grow "in spirit and in truth."

All reality has its deepest meaning in the reality of God, just as the image has its deepest meaning in the object which it proclaims.

When a man breaks away from his spiritual moorings he tears himself from the deeps and goes to the surface, and he becomes more and more superficial. When he loses the spiritual center of Being he loses his own at the same time. And so false centers are formed at the periphery of his life; that is why he becomes progressively superficial. Forced to wander about on the surface of life, cut off from all communion with the energizing, divinizing source of life, he will have to do what he can with his own effective powers; he may create profusely for a while, but in the end he will be drained, exhausted. Only the spiritual man, striking his roots deep in infinite and eternal life, can create a world or preserve a world for men to live wholesome lives in. The uprooted man, despite his extraordinary and stunning scientific performances, sometimes, indeed, because of them (there is glaring evidence of this today), finds himself defenseless amid unbridled elements and menacing natural forces.

Rootlessness leads to ruthlessness. A man without spiritual bearings is an unbalanced man making crazy gesticulations in the air, catching at mere nothings, doing impossible and unreasonable things to get his feet back on the ground. But the ground he needs is the ground of the soul where the Spirit dwells. Until he digs in that far he will be a prey to the devastating forces of the temporal and the earthly. His reforms will cut, purge, and scour; but they will not cure.

Without Spirit, man is but dust and chaff: the action of the Spirit raises him above his nature and introduces him into God's way of life. This Holy Spirit is the power of God who does great things through feeble men. This Spirit continually carries out God's work, which is the building up of the Church and the conversion of the world. It fills our age; it permeates the hearts of men; it needs only to be stirred up.

The proper work of the Spirit is to create grace and so divinize human beings. He transports us into God's sphere.

As a truly divine power He acts in history to bring about the transfiguration of the world. The Spirit is the living and active soul of the Church, building up the mystical Christ through the course of the centuries.

Man, created by the breath of God according to the image and likeness of God, is also a spirit—an embodied spirit. In this spirit, too, he must be rooted. In other words, he must be spiritual.

The origins of the American mind were not predominantly spiritual. The displacements and disassociations of the Protestant uprooting (Reformation) made this impossible. The migrations to the New World were an effect of this state of mind. The old culture of the Middle Ages had broken down; the tradition endured, but sporadically, intermittently, ineffectually. Men's interests became externalized and abstract. They fixed their attention on some narrow aspect of experience, and they pushed that to the limit. Intelligent people were forced to choose between a genuine culture that was old and complete but imperfectly evolved, and a new, rootless culture which, in origin, was thin, partial, abstract, and deliberately indifferent to man's proper interests. The groups that were most completely uprooted were most ready for the American adventure: they turned themselves easily to the mastery of the external environment. To them matter alone mattered. They became completely absorbed in what are still the dominant abstractions and myths of our own time: money, matter, and political rights.

Man, with his severed roots was left spiritless, meaningless, and vacant. To be spiritless means to be susceptible to any form, however unworthy or contrary to nature. This is obviously true to anyone who remembers the nature of a spirit, which is a being with such a tenacious hold on its own nature that it can never become some other thing. To be vacant means, inevitably, to become feverishly and endlessly active: a suicide attempt to fill the vacancy with work, busy work, that fatigues the body and diverts the mind from things that should enrich it. This sort of externalism characterized the growth of our nation. It was aided by politics, which became, in fact, the life of the people; and the national state became their religion. The flag, as Professor Carlton Hayes has shown, supplanted the cross, and the Fathers of the Constitution the Fathers of the Church.

Having become detached from the old culture and commenced a new one, *in vacuo,* the externalizing of interest, the ruthless exploitation of the physical environment was a natural consequence.

To be uprooted from the spirit is to be unhinged. This loose, keelless condition precludes stability and continuity, and leads quite easily to extremes. It is not hard to see why this is so. Any extremity is matter, because spirit always transcends the limitations of the extreme. That is why the principle *in medio stat virtus* does not approve of mediocrity; on the contrary, it demands the deepest commitment to the spiritual. When one chooses a mediocre way of life or task he is rooted in matter, which is always confined to this particularity, to the here-and-now, to a limited and narrow existentialism. Only spirit is outside the limitations of the here-and-now, and can, to that extent, be in contact with and draw from the extremities. It is only by being in the middle that one can touch both extremes.

Only with roots in the spirit, therefore, particularly in the Spirit, that embraces (contains) all things, can we renew the face of the earth.

Since the Holy Spirit is perfect, illimitable, incomprehensible, eternal, and infinite, we need to preserve our roots in mystery: not in something we can know nothing about, but in something we can know more and more about without boredom or drudgery, and without end. A mystery, in short, is an invitation and an enticement to the mind. It offers in itself an inexhaustible realm of Truth into which we can go deeper and deeper, never coming to the end, but discovering immense and immeasurable satisfaction with every step into the depths.

A man needs to live and move in this kind of mystery; otherwise he dries up, stagnates, becomes stale; and he loses his zest for life in the face of a dull, drab, matter-of-fact existence. Religion, precisely because it is mysterious, is crammed with excitement, adventure, and exploration. Rob it of its mystery and you make drab what ought to be dramatic. The mystery of it all keeps us on our toes, makes us alive and alert, induces us to stretch to the full-bodied stature of a man by reaching out infinitely beyond human reach into the very Godhead. The modern "religious revival" is devoid of mystery; it is, therefore, a pathetically feeble, fragile, barren thing. That is why the staggering statistics about a return to religion can be so unimpressive. And they will remain unimpressive as long as religion remains unmysterious, that is to say: man-conscious, self-regarding, full of safe, neat, respectable pathways that lead always into human circles, human interests, human profits. It will remain ineffectual as long as it is merely a department of culture, with a special place reserved for it—a very small one. It must again become all, the force which transfigures and irradiates the whole life from within: its spiritual energy must be set free to change the world.

There is a very specific notion of mystery that needs to be preserved and adhered to. It is the notion found so profusely in the New Testament vocabulary and the apostolic writings. It refers, in one way or another, to the process whereby the inaccessible God is made accessible to men.

Revelation and preaching are concerned first and foremost with mystery. The Apostles are dispensers of mystery: "We speak the wisdom of God in a mystery" (1 Cor 2:7). The deacons bear the mystery about with them in a clean conscience: "Let a man so account of us as of the ministers of Christ, and the dispensers of the mysteries of God" (1 Cor 4:1). This mystery fills the Church and through the Church is made manifest to heaven and earth: "That the manifold wisdom of God may be made known to the principalities and powers in heavenly places through the Church, according to the eternal purpose, which he made, in Christ Jesus our Lord" (Eph 3:10–11).

It is into this mystery we must sink our roots—the mystery of God, which is the plan and economy of salvation, conceived and hidden in God, but made manifest and working by and in Christ Jesus, in the Church and by the preaching of the Apostles. This mystery is broad and wide; it has infinite ramifications; it lies at the heart of everything. All of our Christian endeavors—our liturgy, our mysticism, our apostolate—ought to grow out of it and return to it.

An awareness of historical values is essential to the pursuit of truth. It is ignorance of tradition that causes the rupture and separation of essentially united things, such as service of God and of neighbor, liturgy and contemplation, worship and the apostolate, nature and grace, knowledge and love, asceticism and mysticism.

Philosophy, too, has ceased to be the love of truth, the spirit of wonder in the presence of being, and has been cut up into artificially isolated and unrelated compartments.

All forms of tradition must be received respectfully, reasonably, judiciously. Sacred tradition, which is the innermost core of all tradition, must be received and passed along unaltered because it comes from a divine source, because each generation of men needs to stand on the shoulders of its predecessor, and no individual genius can add anything valid of his own.

In our Western world Christian doctrine is the only tradition of this kind. This tradition can be found obscurely even in the ancient world, in the pre-Christian and non-Christian mythical traditions. It can also be found, thanks to our modern psychological explorations into hidden depths of the personality, in the mysterious place where subconscious certainties abide. This recent knowledge of psychology corroborates St. Augustine's concept of memory: a force capable of clearing a path back through the generations and recalling experiences of mankind at the dawn of history.

Theology is the science of tradition. But, as Josef Pieper wrote in the *Review of Politics* (1958), "theology can fulfill its function as interpreter of the divine word only if it also brings to bear on its task everything else that is known about the world and men. . . ."

When philosophy includes sacred tradition within its sphere, it acquires the stuff of existential importance and urgency. This is the only way that a philosophy can stay alive throughout the centuries, improve the minds of men, and have a favorable impact on society. Today, unfortunately, philosophical discussions eliminate the contents of tradition, and, as a consequence, face the desolating threat of absurdity and despair.

Agreeing with the keen and objective observations of two contemporary philosophers, Karl Jaspers and Gerhard Kreuger, Pieper says: "The unity of the human race is ultimately rooted in the common possession of tradition in its strict sense, in common participation, in the holy tradition that harks back to the word of God."

A man or a race of men without roots in tradition becomes a prey to fancy, whim, caprice, human respect, uninformed popular opinion, emotional reaction, and to whatever is presently in vogue. One of the most deplorable results of this defection from tradition is a type of thinking that poses as the very quintessence of tradition but is, in fact, subtly, and devastatingly, diametrically opposed to tradition. It uses the dogmas of the Church as pillows to sleep on. It takes a vital, resilient, and ever developing tradition and ossifies it so that it becomes something static and incapable of growth. It is insensitive and impervious to the statement of Pius XII that: "the Mystical Body of Christ, as the members who constitute it, does not muffle itself in the abstract, outside the fluctuation of time and space; it is not and cannot be separated from the world which surrounds it. It is always of its age, advancing with it." It is obvious to all, particularly members of religious communities, what happens when authentic tradition is destroyed or ignored: men cling even more desperately to petrified (sometimes stultifying) customs which camouflage as tradition within their isolated groups.

We are called "Catholic" not only because we preach our tradition to all nations, but also because the tradition we preach embraces all cultures and civilizations, leaving its imprint on all things. Our tradition, to be worthy of the name, must touch and color all areas of human life and thought. Our God is the God of all.

One of the most distressing features of uprooted man is the fact that when he loses sight of tradition he loses his hold on the natural law.

Natural law is a term that is easily misunderstood and

misused. It is loaded with ambiguities. So we must be careful to assert here what it is exactly that man must be rooted in. Strictly speaking, it is nothing more than the fundamental rules of human behavior. It is what a modern psychologist, Dr. Oswald Schwarz, less ambiguously calls "essential morality."

This means, generally speaking, that all men recognize that reasonable behavior is morally good; that moderation in regard to food and sex is morally good. But the concrete forms that the moral virtues will take in different cultures or in different times will vary according to historical, geographic, economic, and other circumstances.

The strange variety of facts that sociologists come up with are not moral facts but sociological facts which modify or interfere with the moral fact.

Dr. Frederick E. Flynn, head of the department of philosophy at the College of St. Thomas, St. Paul, Minnesota, concludes:

In our modern pluralist society, with its diversity of religious beliefs, there is only one ground for moral unanimity and that is natural law. Pedants in ivory towers, with academic axes of their own to grind, may invite us to abandon natural law as a basis for moral action. And yet despite these academic attacks, the natural law, as someone once observed, has many times buried its undertakers. Its robustness is man's guarantee of moral growth, for if man ever were really to succeed in burying the natural law, he would at the same time bury with it the guiding plot of the moral drama which makes life human.*

That this condition prevails in America and how it incapacitates us is asserted and explained by Walter Lippmann in his compelling and provocative book: *The Public Philosophy*. It might help to incorporate his thinking here:

Because human nature is, as Hocking puts it, "the most plastic part of the living world, the most adaptable, the most educable," it is also the most maladaptable and miseduca-

* As reported in *The Catholic Messenger*, Davenport, Iowa.

ble. That is why so much depends upon whether or not the wisdom of the good life in a good society is transmitted.

That is the central and critical condition of the Western society: that the democracies are ceasing to receive the traditions of civility, in which the good society, the liberal, democratic way of life at its best, originated and developed. They are cut off from the public philosophy and the political arts which are needed to govern the liberal democratic society. They have not been initiated into its secrets, and they do not greatly care for as much of it as they are prepared to understand. In Toynbee's terrible phrase, they are proletarians who are "in" but are not "of" the society they dominate.†

The public philosophy is a body of positive principles and precepts which a good citizen cannot deny or ignore. This is known as natural law. Without these working principles it is impossible to reach intelligible and workable conceptions of democratic government. Mr. Lippmann's contention is that, increasingly, the people are alienated from the inner principles of their institutions. And what he is worried about is whether and, if so, how modern man can make vital contact with the lost traditions of civility.

Modern men will first need to be convinced that the traditions of civility were not abandoned because they became antiquated. This is one of the roots of their unbelief and there is no denying its depths. . . . The ancient world, we may remind ourselves, was not destroyed because the traditions were false. They were submerged, neglected, lost. For the men adhering to them had become a dwindling minority who were overthrown and displaced by men who were alien to the traditions, having never been initiated and adopted into them. May it not be that while the historical circumstances are obviously so different, something like that is happening again?‡

We need the old ideas; not as such; but reminted. We need a stable, solid frame of reference out of which we can

† From *The Public Philosophy* by Walter Lippmann (p. 75), Copyright 1955, by Walter Lippmann, by permission of Atlantic-Little, Brown and Company, publishers.

‡ *Ibid.*, pp. 80, 81.

establish rational order. We need to work out a body of specific principles and precepts to regulate international relations, and to cope with the problems consequent upon the industrial revolution and the advance of science and technology. We do not need to turn back to the Middle Ages. But we do need goals that are beyond our physical reach, and powers that are stronger and saner than our own. What we ought to remember about the Middle Ages is, as Christopher Dawson reminds us, that the age was an age of faith, not simply because of external religious profession, nor (even less) because men were more moral or more human or more just then than men are today; but rather because men of that age put their faith not in themselves or in human effort, but in something more than civilization and something outside history.

Without such goals and aspirations, without a public philosophy we shall be, as Karl Jaspers says, men dissolved into "an anonymous mass" because we are "without an authentic world, without provenance or roots," without, that is to say, belief and faith that we can live by.

Grace, which is the touch of God's triune, personal love for the human person, works with nature toward a full-grown, divinely enriched personality. The economy of redemption is so erected that a man must fulfill his nature—must be a thinking, loving, feeling thing—if he is to be an adequate working foundation for grace. The more perfectly developed nature is, the more perfectly will it fulfill its destiny of supporting grace. Nature is the interior principle of human movement while grace is the external principle. It is in specifically human action, divinized by grace, that we discover the continuity of nature and grace, where human nature is not destroyed like the eye by the brilliance of light, but led on graciously to the supernature which is the superperfection of man. Man becomes as God.

But since original sin, human nature is no integral and integrated nature waiting simply for the divine influence to protect it. Grace has to deal with a nature that is disintegrated and casual. This state of fallen nature cannot be satisfactorily treated as long as man is regarded individually, in isolation. His mode of acting is profoundly modified by the fact that he is not an isolated kind of creature. He has been made by God as part of the whole creation. So with the fall of man it was the whole "creature" that suffered and began from that moment to "groan and travail waiting for the redemption of man." "Mother Nature" was injured by her human child in an act of disobedient pride, and so it is "Nature," in the general sense of that word, that needs the healing remedy of grace.

In a very thorough study of the roots of religion, Father Conrad Pepler, English Dominican, writes:

Man's potentiality for super-perfection is therefore modified by his being the sinful and disintegrated center of an intricate congeries of creatures which St. Paul calls the *ktisis*. And the healing love of God goes out to man and makes him lovable and a friend in this setting. The Incarnation is grace made physical, the Word made flesh; and Christ completes and fulfills in his person and in the system of the Church and sacraments all the powers and movements of fallen, creaturely man. Grace perfects this nature, so grace comes to man by bread eaten at a sacrificial meal, by water poured from the river over his head, by the tree of the cross, and by the Son of Man hanging thereon. The soul of the individual man is the proper subject of grace, and it works through the infinite potentialities of mind and will; but the individual man is not an isolated point, some choice gem selected by God and removed from the crown of glory in which it is set. Man is perfected by God insofar as he lives and moves in God's universe. . . . A man made whole by Christ's grace is harmonised in himself, harmonised with his fellow human beings, and harmonised with all creation.*

The religion established by Jesus Christ has roots that are fixed in nature; it is a religion which espouses the multitudinous facets of man's nature, and which treats man as a member of a whole gamut of natures we refer to as Mother Nature. This natural religion (in the sense that it is based on man's nature) has ceased to have a compelling grip on

* Conrad Pepler, *Riches Despised* (St. Louis: B. Herder Book Co., 1957), pp. 13–14.

man since he has turned into an unnatural creature by historic factors, principally industrialism.

The ancient religion of the pagans grew out of their natural dependence upon the life-giving or life-withholding spirits that surrounded them. Fire, water, soil, and the rhythm of the seasons provided the inspiration and character of their worship. The Israelites, too, derived their attitudes of worship from the rhythm of the spheres and the seasons, from the elemental dependence of man upon nature and her Author. The roots of their religion were fastened deep and sure into the lifelong heritage from Adam. The "God of Israel" was only the abbreviated form for the God of Abraham, the God of Isaac, and the God of Jacob. The continuity of life from their ancestry assured them of their rightful place and part in the universe. The words of God in Scripture are full of nature. Our Lord speaks mostly about ordinary, commonplace, country things, such as the sowers and their seed, figs and thistles, wheat and weeds, vineyards and laborers, lilies, grass, and sparrows. The lives of natural men will always abound with these. It is only when man pulls up these roots that the natural, traditional symbols of religion lose their meaning and significance.

It is because of the uprootedness of man in this cellophane age that the liturgy—sacrifice, sacrament, and sacramental —has become for the people so complicated, lifeless, and insignificant. Even the born Catholic brought up in Catholic schools needs to have the actions and words of the Mass explained over and over. This recurrent necessity to explain creates at the heart of worship a classroom atmosphere—the last thing in the world to appeal to simple worshipers from factory and office. The whole of human existence is so dependent upon mechanism and techniques that even the simple action of Christian worship has, now, the earmarks of a professional technique.

This false dichotomy between the ritual and natural levels of a man's life cripples his art and culture. It also forces him to worship through a medium wrapped around with artificiality. This is one reason why the average man is not easily attracted to liturgical functions, and why there has to be so much external pressure expended toward getting the people to enter into the spirit of the liturgy. For the same reason many people are led into artificially contrived "ways of perfection" without ever thinking of linking them to the worship of the Church, and the liturgical cycle. To quote Pepler once again:

The center of the problem lies not with the liturgy itself but with the life of the average man who, apart from those few minutes spent in church, is carried along by a tide that flows in a direction contrary to the full human worship of God. The Christian is "naturally" swept along by this tide; the current that goes Godward is "unnatural" to him. For that reason the struggle to maintain a liturgical atmosphere has become self-conscious and highly rationalized, and cerebral, whereas all around the worshipper the things of God's creation praise Him inevitably, naturally.*

The break with nature is most evident, perhaps in the disorder of the imagination, which should be expected since the imagination is the bridge between sense and sensibility. One's mental equipment depends upon the furniture of the imagination or the pictures of human experience that have been retained. When society becomes entirely secular and mechanized, men's common experience and imaginative furniture become secular. And so the Pope speaks:

The Church cannot overlook that what is driving away from her a notable portion of the working world is exactly that which is alienating from her souls in the other classes of humanity; and that is the deterioration of anemic minds, emptied of all spiritual and religious impulse, victims of an epidemic, which is ravaging so many, many men today. They are phantoms of men, who, never tired of frequenting cinemas and sports field, day and night filled with futile novelties, of popular illustrations, of light music, are too empty to take an interest in occupying themselves from their own resources.

This confirms the problem we were dealing with a moment ago; integrating worship into our daily, ordinary, twentieth-century lives. The problem is thornier and more

* *Op. cit.,* p. 81.

complicated than many liturgical enthusiasts would care to admit; and the problem arises because man today is on the whole an industrialized, uprooted man. Perhaps our first efforts lie in the much more fundamental endeavor of trying to reestablish roots.

One of the greatest blessings of our modern technology, our American economic system, our productivity is the new leisure they have given our people. Golden hours of one's own have been added to each day, days to each week, years to each lifetime.

But the ironic, even tragic, part of this boon to good living is that few have learned how to use this new leisure. The average American is uneasy even when he tries to relax. The qualities that were indispensable in creating our standard of living become a formidable handicap when he seeks to enjoy his hard-won leisure.

Communication, with which the modern man is obsessed, kills the art of communion by which man is enriched and ennobled. Communication starts by being an aid, a convenience. It grows, grows, grows—like a tree if you like it, like a cancer if you don't. In any case, it ends as a way of life. The transmission and reception of messages, almost irrespective of meaning, becomes an activity fascinating in itself. It can be quite satisfying, though never fulfilling, to certain temperaments that are outgoing, social, manipulative, present-minded. But it yields its last measure of satisfaction only if pushed to its last degree of development. This involves an assault on privacy or, rather, a common, unconscious willingness to be assaulted.

Boredom and ennui, a frantic search for diversion are the common reactions to an hour, or a day of quiet. The modern Cleopatra in Eliot's *Wasteland* desperately asks: "What shall I do? . . . What shall we do tomorrow? What shall we ever do?" She expresses one of contemporary man's most pathetic problems. Publishers of pornography and pap, producers of endless third-rate movies and TV programs have made their fortunes providing an answer—false but lucrative.

There is a compulsion, also, to keep on the move. What would happen to the vacation traveler if he were to linger on somewhere long enough to open the possibility of perceiving and understanding? What keeps the tourist "on the go" is emptiness and incapacity, inability to fill a pause in the day's occupation with anything worth doing: justified fear of leisure time. The radio and television industries are based on the assumption that the American people are so poor in personal resources that they must have entertainment available at the turn of a switch twenty-four hours a day.

Our lives revolve—in quiet desperation—around our work. This is killing. Inhuman is the man who is fettered to the process of work. Any man whose life is completely filled by his work shrinks inwardly and contracts, with the result that he can no longer act significantly outside his work, and perhaps can no longer even conceive of such a thing.

Home education is important. Enforced leisure (the child made to stay alone as a punishment) develops a distaste for aloneness that may last a lifetime. The child who whines: "I've got no one to play with," "nothing to do," must learn delight from his parent's joyous example: "I've got a whole hour, or a whole day, how wonderful." If a child sees only a bustling parent, hiding from himself in his own murky flatulence, always finding ways to while away the time or to kill it by Scrabble, TV, golf, or idle, small-time chatter, the child, too, will dribble away, like a leaking faucet, all of himself except the superficial.

A child favorably impressed with leisure may, indeed, reap precious fruit from even enforced solitary confinement later on. Prophets, philosophers, and saints have achieved wonders in jail. It is always a mistake for the enemies of a dynamic man to lock him up or to confine him in any way. As Pandit Nehru, who knows, said: "it gives him enforced leisure to read and think—the sources of real power." The sources are valid for saints and scoundrels alike. Would it not be wiser for their enemies to leave them at large to work off their steam in a life of action than to jail them where they concentrate on manufacturing intellectual time bombs?

Humanity is seldom made to look more foolish than it makes itself by acts of persecution. Time inevitably has the laugh on it, and a grim laugh it is. The case histories bear

this out. Take Boethius: lying in prison at Pavia while awaiting execution (A.D. 524) he writes a book which makes him
schoolmaster to Europe for centuries, *The Consolations of
Philosophy*. Cervantes wrote *Don Quixote* in jail. John Bun-
yan lay in the dungeon of Bedford Gaol when he could have
had his liberty at any time if he had promised to give up
preaching. As a consequence, *Pilgrim's Progress* goes on
preaching for hundreds of years to people of all nations,
races, and religions. One of the greatest pieces of religious
literature in the world was written by St. John of the Cross.
Most of this was done in prison. The list of masterpieces
written in jail is exceeded only by those written in exile.
Mohammed flees for his life from Mecca and in desert wan-
derings dictates the *Koran*. Athens banishes one of her gen-
erals, Thucydides, for his failure in an expeditionary cam-
paign; and he writes his incomparable *History*. Euripides goes
into voluntary exile in Macedonia where he writes his most
poetic tragedy, the *Bacchae*. While the Florentines sought
Dante to burn him alive, he wrote, in exile, the *Divine Com-
edy*. And on and on—right down to our own Concord solitary,
Henry David Thoreau.

So beware of the dynamic thoughtful man in exile or in
jail. Jail means a stoppage of traffic. If one's normal traffic
flow of ideas, two-way, pro and con, give and take, is stopped
by a dead-end block of suspicion, hatred, slander, persecution, jealousy, prejudice, legalism, formalism, false witness,
envy, authoritarianism, he is as effectively in jail as though
locked up.

"Liberty means responsibility. That is why most men dread
it." Dreading liberty, persecutors would deny it to others.
And yet persecution is so terribly shortsighted. It may be a
complete immediate success, only to destroy for centuries to
come the present good or bad condition of the nation, the
community, the superior that allows it to be practiced.

Our school system is partly responsible for our incapacity
for leisure. *Schola* means "leisure," but all leisure has been
deliberately squeezed out of school. So education has increased our will to professionalize, to specialize (even our
sports and games), leaving us incurious about any intellec-

tual or sensuous experience that a specialist cannot put to use.

In differing degrees, we are all born with the same senses and potentialities. When we who enjoyed painting in kindergarten grow up, nothing has happened to deny us the same satisfaction (though not necessarily the same excellence) that Abraham Rattner gets at an easel—nothing except that the faculty was allowed to atrophy from disuse.

As children we also enjoyed dancing and singing, but as we went on through school we learned that nothing was worth learning unless it had pragmatic value and advanced our specialization. If our schools provided leisure, we would be less specialized but more original, creative, and versatile. Fewer of us would be pros and more of us amateurs. But we would be ourselves; and we would be whole, happy, and really alive. And we would make a greater contribution to the world. St. Thomas said that it is necessary for the perfection of human society that there should be men who devote their lives to contemplation. Unfortunately most of us do not have the simple wisdom of Melanie, the little child of La Salette, who said she didn't want to go to school because there was so much noise "and I'm afraid my heart might hear it."

The significance of the amateur is that his sport is to no end but itself. It is pursued solely for an enjoyment beyond which there is no end except excellence. However slight the excellence, however limited his capacity to refine or increase it, the amateur's reward is that he has done what he can without usefulness or practical gain.

Apart from making a living, the average specialized pro has found no zest for life. Except in relation to his job, his mind is color-blind, tone-deaf, and mute. Inborn faculties whose use would create gusto and delight have fossilized. He remains commonplace and incurious, with no passion for learning or understanding. His is the common lot of us all. No wonder we are bored—and bores. No wonder that leisure scares us.

This basic indisposition for leisure is unfortunate because the basis of human perfectibility is free time. Now that we are liberated from the practical, workaday world, from the welter of ordinary, undistinguished things, from the tangible, unrefined elements of life, from our puritan-inherited concepts of morality—Idleness is the devil's workshop; hand work is man's salvation, etc.—now that we are free, are we going to fritter away our heritage reading the comics, or, in some equally childish manner, wasting time?

Science has led us to the pinnacle of human possibilities but has not added a single cubit of wisdom to our lives. That is our inescapable responsibility. It poses, in fact, the biggest problem of modern man—perhaps even bigger than war: what to do with himself. As he ceases to be a creature of endless toil, he is likely to find himself liberated into a vacuum. His leisure time can become more of a curse than the plagues of old.

For leisure by itself does not mean progress. It need not be of itself purposeful. It does not of itself make visible new horizons or lead to deeper human fulfillment. It is as neutral as the time of day. It can set the stage for meaningless distractions, expunging and consuming man's awareness and sensitivity, thus depriving him of his uniqueness as a man.

What, then, is education asked to do? What is its biggest job in an age of leisure? The making of a new man—someone who has confidence in the limitless possibilities of his own development, someone who is not intimidated by the prospect of an open hour, someone who is aware that science may be able to make an easier world but only man can make a better one.

What will save leisure from whiling away man's time and make it the most fruitful thing man has yet known? Contemplation. Leisure is not merely the interim between the acts of the working life. It is an intense activity but of a different kind. Repose—true leisure—cannot be enjoyed without some recognition of the spiritual world. For the first purpose of repose is the contemplation of the good.

"God saw all that he made and found it very good." Such contemplation of his work is natural to man, wherever he too is engaged in a creative task. We must, like a painter, take time to stand back from our work, to be still, and thus see what's what. St. Thomas Aquinas says that no man can act virtuously unless he sees what's what. And so he needs time to contemplate. True repose is standing back to survey the activities that fill our days.

Repose allows us to contemplate the little things we do in their relation to the vast things which alone give them worth and meaning. Repose gives us time for an intensely active and creative contemplation of divine things from which we arise refreshed.

It is in leisure, genuinely understood, that man rises above the level of a thing to be used and enters the realm where he can be at home with the potentialities of his own nature; where, with no concern for doing, no ties to the immediate, the particular, and the practical, he can attend to the love of wisdom, can begin leading a truly human life.

Plato said it this way: "But the gods, taking pity on mankind, born to work, laid down the succession of recurring feasts to restore them from their fatigue . . . so that nourishing themselves in festive companionship with the gods, they should again stand upright, and erect." The nature of leisure is thus basically united to contemplation, the great tradition of Western culture, and both are dependent on a real awareness of the transcendent and the divine.

The soul of leisure is celebration. When a day is too good to be used, we celebrate it. It becomes a feast. As G. K. Chesterton said: "When man gives God a holy day, God gives man a holiday." Since God is too good to be used, we celebrate His goodness. This is divine worship, which, ultimately, is the only thing that makes leisure possible and justifiable. Divine worship means the same thing where time is concerned, as the temple where space is concerned. "Temple" means that a particular space of ground, a specific building, is withdrawn from utilitarian purposes and given over, dedicated, exclusively, to the presence and purposes of God. Similarly in divine worship, a certain definite space of time is set aside from working hours and days, a limited time, specially marked off and not used—withdrawn from all utilitarian ends.

It is in this atmosphere of worshipful leisure that man oversteps the frontiers of the everyday workaday world, not in external effort and strain, but as though lifted above it in ecstasy. That is the meaning of sacrament: a visible sign of a deeper, unseen reality. A sacrament should lift man out of himself, so that he is rapt to the heavens. Let no one imagine for a moment that that is a private and romantic interpretation. The Church has pointed to the meaning of the Incarnation of the Word in the selfsame words: "that we may be rapt into love of the invisible reality through the visibility of that first and ultimate sacrament—the Incarnation."

It is, therefore, through this kind of leisure, holy repose, this kind of divine worship, of celebration of the liturgy, that man, who is "born to work," is drawn out of himself, out of the toil and moil of every day into the sphere of unending holiday; drawn out of the confined sphere of work and labor into the heart and center of creation.

Cut off from the worship of the Divine, leisure becomes laziness and work inhuman. Although leisure does, indeed, embrace everything which, without being merely useful, is an essential part of a full human existence, its deepest source, by which it is fed and continues to be vital, is the celebration of divine worship.

There is one institution in the world, thank God, which forbids useful activity and servile work on particular days, and in this way prepares a sphere for a real, dignified human existence. The Church, through her Mass, sacraments, and cycle of feasts, invites man to that leisure and contemplation where he can again "stand upright and erect." It provides one of the last remaining refuges from a busy, restless world.

The contemplative spirit, born and nurtured in the sacramental life of the Church, needs for its full growth copious supplies of solitude and silence absolutely indispensable ingredients of leisure. Much more is involved than simple withdrawal from the society of men and the cessation of speech.

Solitude means being full of God, being drawn into the amiable society of the Three Persons of the Trinity; and although this means, sometimes, absolute seclusion, at other times it simply means self-possession, including the possession of God, on the busy streets and during the most crowded moments of a lifetime. But we seem to be capable of the latter only after we have resorted deliberately and frequently enough to periods of absolute aloneness.

In all ages, God has formed in solitary places the great contemplatives and the instruments of His great works. Moses goes into the desert alone where God manifests Himself and makes Moses the leader of the Hebrew people. It is after walking for forty days in the desert that Elias, on the desolate mountain of Horeb, hears the gentle whisper that reveals the divine Presence. John the Baptist is drawn into the desert by the weight of the singular grace received on the day of the Visitation of our Lady. Not until the age of thirty does he leave it, filled with the spirit of God and ready to accomplish his mission as precursor. St. Paul, after his conversion, retires into Arabia; and under the direct action of the Holy Spirit, prepares for his special mission in the apostolate. Out of solitude come the great bishops of the first centuries to build our Christian civilization. Later St. Ignatius of Loyola receives, during his year of solitude at Manresa, the lights that permit him to write the book of *Spiritual Exercises*, and to organize the Society of Jesus. And the Order of Carmel, which has given the Church her great mystical doctors, had its birth in the desert. There it lives, or at least it returns there incessantly for the atmosphere which can provide for its attractions and the development of its life.

And so it is in solitude that man most readily and frequently encounters God and becomes divinely empowered to be an apostle. But even from the purely natural point of view man needs solitude. Without it his natural life suffers serious vitamin deficiency. The shallowness which stultifies so much of the existence around us comes from a lack of privacy, of quiet, of solitude. Solitude is the nurse of full-grown men, and is as needful to humanity as society. The human animal consists of three living components: the body, the mind, and the soul. Each must be sustained, each must be given its food, its exercise, and its pleasures. For an individual to learn how to provide the necessities of life to his own three components is to learn the secret of constructive solitude.

To go into solitude is not to blank the mind; it is to rest it. The mind truly at rest is, as Disraeli pointed out, "the nurse of enthusiasm and enthusiasm is the true parent of genius. In all ages solitude has been called for—has been flown to."

There is a German word—*Sammlung*—for which there is no explicit single word translation in English. It means a collecting, a marshaling of forces. It could be the label for that gathering of forces, that time of solitude and mind rest when a great speaker, actor, or poet shuts out everything but the mood at hand.

In self-integration of this sort we are not really negating the world around us. We are rather getting ourselves and the world into focus. Out of the scrap basket of a day's small frazzlements we are putting together a time of containment and a time of strength.

Solitude, then, is as necessary for human sanctity and sanity as is human fellowship. But it is much harder to acquire. In twentieth-century living, the mind at rest—solitude —is brought by a discipline exercised by few and fewer people. The physical and material surroundings of the century don't encourage it. The newly designed house provides an almost automatic short circuit to contemplation. The private den has become the public TV room. The dining room is an open area. Kitchens are no longer cozy but efficient; gone is the comfortable chair which once invited a small time of reflection for Mother while dinner vegetables bubbled softly on the stove. In most contemporary houses there are no hidden rooms upstairs and far away from the noise; the hustle and bustle of ordinary, leveling "togetherness." Even the doors between rooms are eliminated; and with them has gone the last slamming refuge of an outraged child and the easiest automatic means for ensuring a time of repose to "repair our nature" as Shakespeare's King Henry VIII put it.

So we must fight for solitude, for the right to be alone, to be still and know God, to be quiet and thoughtful and see things as they really are. Toward this end we must construct each day, plan it, live it, refuse to be inundated by it or dehumanized by it in any way. In the budget of hours, whether it's a lifetime or a day, there is room for whatever we want to create, but we must take the means of creativity which are at hand and work with them. Every day can have its peak, as Goethe reminded us, "on every mountain height is rest."

Besides the positive cultivation of solitude within the realm of leisure, man needs to develop interior silence. Serious-minded men, magnanimous men, are necessarily men of silence.

What was it that kept the Mother of God silent most of her life? There was something in her so sacred, so absorbing, magnificent, and compelling that it left no room, time, or energy for much verbiage. She was filled with the Word of God. All she could do was listen. She tells us so herself: she spent her days pondering on the meaning of the words of her divine Son. And so she was the woman wrapped in silence. She was absorbed and held captive by the power and the glory of the Word made flesh.

What happened to John the Baptist when Christ appeared on the scene? He was the last towering figure of the old world. He was a mighty defender of the rights of God, a rugged, masculine character if ever there was one. His voice was strong and relentless, crying in the wilderness: make straight the way of the Lord. And it was heard; it made a universal impression, an ineluctable one. But when Christ came, John ceased to raise his voice. He kept silence.

Why? Because John was a stouthearted man, a man apart, with a single eye. He wanted just one single joy, one unique pleasure: the incomparable joy and pleasure of hearing the voice of His Beloved. And he gave up everything else for that. He became silent in order to listen with all his might to the voice of Christ. "And no man ever spoke like this man." Even his enemies claimed this.

Why do we sometimes, on a purely natural level, find it difficult to speak? It is because we are deeply engaged; our minds are gripped; our hearts are full. It is for the same reason that we find it impossible to do two important things at once. We cannot solve intricate mathematical problems and play tennis at the same time.

When we are preoccupied with God we are bound to be silent. God invades the privacy of our souls filling our imaginations, intellects, and wills. We are compelled to be silent. So silence is not a negation. It is an absorption, a recollection; it is a Christian inwardness: being drawn deeper and deeper into the ground of the soul where we are confronted with ultimate reality, with God; it is listening with all our might to the Word of God. God has spoken. His Word was made flesh.

We must learn to use the leisure with which we are already blessed. And we must make a colossal, untiring effort to introduce more and more holy repose into our lives.

Youthful radicalism has not vanished. It abounds more plentifully than ever before in every nook and cranny of America. It does tend to fizzle and evaporate though.

The question is, then: Why does youthful radicalism fizzle and evaporate? It seems to me that it does so primarily because of a dearth of adult leadership. The radical potential is left untapped, uneducated; it is even purposely smothered. It is smothered by our *crowd culture,* our *superficial religion,* our *monstrous schools,* our worship of the *common man,* and our unreasonable yen for *conformity.*

A *culture* is a composition of attitudes and resultant actions in which are embodied and revealed the prevailing aspirations and desires of that group of human beings amid which one lives. American culture is a crowd culture, provincial and dangerously trivial. How can we expect youth to be impervious to the dehumanizing influence of a cultural environment?

There is within them a capacity for nobleness and greatness, but it is a very tender plant. They lose their high aspirations as they lose their intellectual taste. This happens because they have not time or opportunity for indulging them; and they addict themselves to inferior pleasures because they are either the only ones to which they have access, or the only ones which they are any longer capable of enjoying.

And if inferior pleasures are so accessible, is it not an adult fault? Is not our present cult of the common man an adult creation? And is it possible to have an age of the common man without having an age of the common denominator? Once such an age is established, we should not be surprised to find our young people deadening themselves on inferior pleasures produced by us and our new powerful media gunned at mass appeal.

And so you have the pulp magazines, the digests, the sensational mammoth monthlies, and all the other written stuff consumed so ravenously by decent people who, by right, ought not even allow such offensive material in their homes. The comic books and strips we supply them with so abundantly are even worse: vulgar, horrible, sentimental, inane. Matthew Arnold said: "If one were searching for the best means to efface and kill in a whole nation the discipline of respect, the feeling for what is elevated, one could not do better than take the American newspaper." Most of the music we compose and the movies we produce tend to defile the young.

A long time ago a man of deep understanding said that humanity's progress lay in fixing attention on whatsoever things are true, honorable, just, lovely, and of good report. Most of the American media of communication seem devoted to fixing public attention on whatsoever things are trivial, ugly, vulgar, salacious, and of ill-report as though they were consciously exploiting for profit the lowest depths of human nature.

Radio, television, and press management not only miss (or insult) the superior portion of humanity, but commit the irreparably harmful mistake of gauging the common man's capacity too low. This is an error which the Catholic press has not been entirely immune to; to which it has, in part, succumbed—to our own loss the shame.

We have made the *Common Man* too common. Of all the unfavorable influences operating within our society and governing the behavior of teen-agers, the most injurious is the tendency to confuse the common denominator with a standard of excellence. This tendency is glaringly exemplified by radio and television which produce what the greatest number of people seem to want. But to confuse the best with what is most widely and most generally acceptable is to reveal a spiritual confusion which is as fundamental as it is subtle and insidious. It could readily bring to naught any solution of the mechanical and economical problems created by the age of mass production.

Our sole standard of value seems to be the opinion of the people. Anything done to satisfy that opinion is all right no matter how wrong, like prostituting the language and assaulting the dignity of the individual.

In the meantime, we deprive youth of their "fifth Freedom"—the freedom to be *themselves,* their best selves, the opportunity of each one of them to develop to his highest power. If only some of us would stand on our toes, and expend our best efforts toward influencing an elite: that larger-than-we-think segment of teen-agers, restless, receptive, and eager for the fullness of life.

If only we would recognize our adult responsibility, we would use our position of influence not to cater obsequiously —with cruel pity—to the crowd; but to be society's leaven rather than its tool. It is our task to sharpen the spirit, to cultivate taste, to develop personality, to save souls for glory, for splendor, for God; not by shaping our efforts to crowd or teen-age apathy or sameness, but to their highest aspirations and distinctness; not by highlighting the lowest common denominator, but by emphasizing the highest.

There ought to be a great deal of devotion, solicitude, and reverence for the common man—but for his manhood and not his commonness. In other words, we ought to be providing every possible opportunity for every young man or woman to become as uncommon and superior as possible.

Our *public education* has thus far been unable to rescue us from what we are. It has itself become the servant of our defective culture, mirroring our modern mistakes and, with zest, encouraging our children to repeat those mistakes.

The common denominator is being exalted, unfortunately not only by the common man himself and his exploiters, but also by those who are supposed to be educators and intellectual leaders. They seek to know not what a good education essentially and necessarily involves but what *most* students want. Instead of using books that are the wisest, best, and most appropriate, they use books that have been proved by the polls to be the most read with the least pain.

There is frequently no fixed standard for marking examination papers, but only a variable goal situated in the neighborhood of the usual level of achievement; and even words unfamiliar to the average student are edited out of the books he is given to read. Courses are planned for and built up around the median of the class. The good student is unchallenged, bored. The loafer sails through undisturbed. And this lack of outstanding students and high standards passes for democracy.

Do we really educate them? We want our young people to be accepted, to get along, to inherit our knack of making money, to share our comfortable existence. And we forget to teach them *who they are* and *where they are going.* So we make them rootless, and a prey to every potential leader of a gang. We drive them to become "rebels without a cause," to espouse idiocy to such an extent as to drive madly, at full speed, off a precipitous cliff for lack of "nothing better to do."

Seminaries, too, need to take stock. Are they producing future leaders? A critic recently wrote: "Too little criticism from outside enters the seminary. Ideas, books, currents of sensibility and thought do not live there reasonably enough." Superiors should not only accept the public opinion of the layman's world, but avidly seek it. Out of a ceaseless, unremitting, but discriminating dialogue between the seminary and the world outside, the student will gain a larger and more real perspective of things as they are and will be prepared to give theology to the people in a way that is fresh, alive, sincere, and effective.

In the January-February, 1960, issue of *Perspectives,* Father John McManmon, C.S.C., wrote that

on the American scene what is commonly called Catholic philosophy and theology is, if not dead, certainly near death. It is dying for lack of the vital life-blood of inspiration and creative disagreement and comparison. American Catholic philosophers and theologians, especially dogmatic theologians, are not only failing their predecessors, but are drawing down undeserved ridicule on their work. To revivify itself, and especially within the seminary, the instinct and know-how for positive and creative thought. Complete abandonment of the findings of the past is foolish; but also foolish is a concept of tradition which defines itself as adherence to the past as past. . . .

Tradition is not past, nor is it in the past; tradition should live, and breathe, and inspire here and now. Tradition was vital and is now vital but only when it is used as a springboard for progress, illumination, and creativity in our exploration of contemporary problems.*

Père Yves Congar, O.P., one of the Church's most distinguished theologians, adds to this statement in the same issue of *Perspectives* that

it is a fact frequently verified that today the exterior forms of the Church draw a veil over not only the Gospel and God, but also over the Church's own proper mystery. The Christian world obscures Christianity. Some would accept the faith readily enough if it were presented simply as it sprang from its sources, but one can scarcely recognize the Gospel under those historic garments which hide its living reality and make it appear foreign to itself. So, frequently, it is from the outside that one discovers the basic value of the Gospel and of the Church herself; or rather, and more happily, it is by discovering and remaining close to the new expressions of faith and of worship, which are being found once more as they spring from their sources. There is here evidence of facts, which I believe, cannot be ignored without passing over one of the clearest directions of the Holy Spirit at the present time.†

Father Bernard Meyer deals with the gap between priest and people in his book, *Lend Me Your Hands*. Speaking of seminary studies in general, he says:

Seminary classes should be so orientated as to make Our Lord's command to His Church the integrating principle of the curriculum. We are not simply training priests as such, but priests with a specific mission. The circumstances and challenges of this mission keep changing. If priestly training does not provide for that, it is like the auto maker who still produces models of thirty years ago. Theology ought to build a bridge between revealed truth and the modern mind, which is so little receptive of abstract ideas. The doctrines of our Faith were not revealed in a nice logical system, but in a

* Notre Dame, Ind.: Fides Publishers.
† Notre Dame, Ind.: Fides Publishers.

personal, human contact, and that is the way we should learn to present them to the people, even though we may need the systematic approach for ourselves.

Dogmatic theology is really the science of love, the study of God's plan to restore the unity of man with God and with his fellow man. Our Lord not only redeemed us, but wanted us to be his co-redeemers. More emphasis needs to be laid on the apostolic work of the Church, so that young priests may catch the vision of bringing lay Christians to play their vital part in God's plan for the restoration of human society to Him. The function of the laity in the Church's mission has been sadly neglected in dogmatic theology, more specifically in the section treating of Christ's Church. The future priest should learn more about the role of parents, the family and Christians according to their state in life for incarnating the world. Because we know so little about this we fail to arm our people against modern social disorganization.

For example, the diocesan clergy in mission lands have sometimes been criticized for not having enough zeal. How can we expect them to imitate the methods of Christ when we look at their seminary training? It is the product of the period when the theological arguments were made necessary by Protestant attacks. We keep repeating all the old arguments to seminarians in Asia and Africa who are far removed from that situation. The more important study of how to reach people is only lightly touched on. The kind of training they need is to be made experts in bringing their people into partnership with Christ in the apostolate. . . .

The mission of the Church is twofold, apostolic and sacramental. Our traditional seminary course, developed originally in Catholic countries, has emphasized the second. The priestly pattern acquired in the seminaries of Europe and America is one of the individual spiritual life and sacramental service, but we have not been taught how to join them with ourselves by apostolic work, which would give the Faith a strong social content as it had in the time of Christ and the early Church. We tend to present it as abstract ideas combined with ritual obligations instead of as the warm love of Christ, the Person, manifested today in the community of priests and Catholics sharing it with others, which could be an irresistible attraction.*

* Notre Dame, Ind.: Fides Publishers, 1955.

Much more could be quoted from Fathers Jungman and Hofinger along the same line, accentuating the need for a "Kerygmatic theology" that would equip the seminarian to give sermons and instructions full of the positive, concrete warmth of the Gospel, the "good news," in a way more suited to the people.

I have resorted to these long and various quotations in order to highlight the fact that the ardent plea for a reformation and refreshment of theological expression is being made all over the world and in high places.

The solution, obviously, is not to scrap or even weaken the scientific courses of theology; the problem may not even be best solved by adding Kerygmatic theology courses to an already crowded curriculum. It may be that the extra year of theology (pastoral), prescribed by the Holy See if planned carefully and executed effectively by *men of wide and varied pastoral experience*, will eventually prove to be the happiest solution.

On the matter of *conformity* this has to be said. Adolescence is the period of transition from the life of the child to that of the adult. It cannot be an easy transition. The adult world we offer them is no enticement. It is hard for them to begin to live with those who crave only for success, who regard their fellowmen merely as means to their selfish ends, whose ways are dark and devious, who have no understanding of frankness and kindness but believe everyone's conduct to be dissimulation, who regard the people in their environment as enemies instead of as fellow workers, who are unable to conceive of any values that are absolute and not relative, because they are the center of their own worlds, who therefore know of nothing more worth striving for than self-exaltation and the changing possibilities of pleasure.

We grownups have isolated "teen-agers" as if they were an especially dangerous group. Categorizing them as such, with the unmistakable connotation of juvenile and delinquent, we brand them, and give them—whether we want to or not—a bad role to play. And so something that formerly plagued only adults is now a stumbling block right in the heart of teen-agedom, namely role identification. This means conformity to teen-ageism—a category created and nurtured by adults.

Two unfortunate things are happening in the meantime. As they rebel against adult conformity, they are driven back into the teen-age gang for strength of resistance, and they blindly conform to it. And their conformity is worse sometimes than ours. They are compelled to wear the same kind of clothes, use the same vocabulary, etc. They would die rather than be regarded by their pals as a drip, a lemon, or a square. This can have furious dehumanizing and demoralizing effects on them as persons, especially if their friends are unknown to their parents.

The second way we have estranged them is by our inattention to them because of our all-out pursuit of the "high-standard American way of life." They have thus become more and more foreign to us, even to their own parents. A recent survey among grade-school boys revealed that the average time spent by each father with each son, per week, is eight minutes.

But what antagonizes them most of all just when they are ready and eager to share our adult life of rich and varied maturity, is what they find to be our lot: a vast and sickly pattern of conformity involving such senseless and un-American behavior as fear and hatred of Negroes, Jews, foreigners, artists, intellectuals, and others; comprising laws that govern the kind of money you make, where you live, your choice of friends, clubs, and such matters.

Many of the nation's wise men stake the health of the society upon consistent adjustment of individuals to the opinion of the group. This is not simply an unwitting desire for conformity, but a philosophy of life. It clips the burgeoning brilliance of our youth. It chokes enthusiasm. It destroys genius. It impedes holy indignation. And so there is no one with a capacity for Olympian laughter, no great tranquil rebels like Christ, no saints who refuse, like uncompromising Gibraltars, to adjust to the capricious temper of the times.

The ideals of the schools, churches, clinics, and societies are all the same: conformity by means of adjustment. Normalcy has almost completely replaced excellence as an ideal.

What about the stable virtues of righteousness, integrity, truth? The question is no longer how one ought to act, but how do most people act. Or as David Riesman sums it up in his brilliant work called *The Lonely Crowd*, the American who used to be conspicuously "inner-directed" is now conspicuously "other-directed."

Must we adjust ourselves to the aims of our present-day culture, which are avowedly ease and material well-being? Or are we required to spend ourselves untiringly in a ceaseless effort to challenge the best that is in our young people and evoke a corresponding response? The answer is obvious. But the reality of it is not present in our country today. Small wonder that Charles Malik, Lebanese delegate to the United Nations, writes: "There is in the West [in the United States] a general weakening of moral fibre. Leadership does not seem to be adequate to the unprecedented challenge of the age." The conduct of 6000 Americans during their Korean imprisonment gave us dreadful evidence of this shocking moral weakness.

It is a bit frightening: conformity is shaping up to something akin to religion. Perhaps we will some day resemble an ant society—through unbridled desire to get along with one another, and be the same as any ordinary good Joe.

A biological axiom explains that progress is made only through differences. The breeders of race horses would have little success if some animals were not born different from the ordinary. The same is true of tulips or tomatoes—or thinkers. If we all tend to think the same way either out of laziness or under compulsion, the laws broadly governing intellectual development cease to operate.

While it is true that many of the young people have abandoned "causes for convertibles," and no longer feel Dante's "divine discontent," may not the whole trend be traced back to adults who live by and preach the principle that it is often safer to conform than it is to become an individual?

The conformist lacks faith. Is not democracy a profession of faith in the individual? Faith not only in one another but in oneself, one's inner resources, the fundamental capacity to dream and create. No man is an island, to be sure. But how John Donne would writhe if he heard who was preaching his little gem today, and why!

It is regrettable and false to think that the healthy system is the one in which the individual feels no conflict. All great and salutary changes and reforms have come about, and always will, because someone was frustrated by the status quo, because someone exercised the skepticism, the questioning, and the kind of curiosity, which, to borrow a phrase, blows the lid off everything.

It is the rebel, the critic, the person alone, who has the ability and stamina to make society and the world better. He is made of pioneer stuff; for the true pioneer, symbol of America, by his very act is a nonconformist.

Religion, as it is practiced by adults, has not adequately shaped the lives of young people. It is much too organized and too little religious for the task. It seeks too avidly its own preservation, at cost of compromise. It does not tell the whole truth about God and man. It is so wrapped around with artificial symbol and complicated ritual that most people never get beyond the threshold, never get to the heart of religion, which is contemplation or religious experience (in the true, deep, theological sense of that expression). Much of the worship of our modern type of religion tends to be pedestrian, and its morality is far too much a sentimentalized worldliness.

One cannot grow spiritually strong on a religion that is man-centered, that seeks immediate material good, that has lost the awesome sense of man facing God, that debases Christianity making it a means to lesser ends—which by its very nature the Christian religion cannot be.

The enlivening of religion depends most of all upon priests and theologians. The priest is the intermediary between man and God; between man who flees and God who pursues; between reluctant man and God omnipotent; between man who moves backward, bent in his weakness, and God who requires all of him in the name of His tenacious and immense love. So much, then, depends upon his leadership, his inspiration.

It is up to him to open young minds to a vision, fix young wills on towering objectives, so structure the atmosphere they breathe that they are forced to run, fly, soar.

It is not enough for the priest to administer the sacraments, and to be friendly with his people, playing games with them—or talking games with them—stirring them, mixing them, and churning the batter: none of this is enough if he leaves out the leaven of the spirit. The priest has got to be, perhaps above all, a spiritual director as personally, directly, and continually as possible.

High school and college students are easily inspired. They live in a wide world of wonder and they are always ready to explore: they are looking for paths and guides and, as Mr. A. P. Campbell wrote in *Spiritual Life* (September, 1958),

they are ever alert for the bugle sound of the hunt. It is a matter of the right bugle sound; and if we do not give them bright and glorious inspiration, they will listen to other horns or make up their own music and ours will not be heard at all. We cannot blame the young if they are rushing like brown rats after Pied Piper Presleys. We have not piped to them ourselves. We have let them wander off into a world barred to us, a world we helped to make for them.

IMAGE BOOKS

IMAGE BOOKS

THE CONFESSIONS OF ST. AUGUSTINE – Translated with an Introduction by John K. Ryan (D101) – $1.75

THE THIRD REVOLUTION: A Study of Psychiatry and Religion – Dr. Karl Stern (D113) – 95¢

A WOMAN CLOTHED WITH THE SUN – Edited by John J. Delaney (D118) – $1.25

INTERIOR CASTLE – St. Teresa of Avila (Translated by E. Allison Peers) – (D120) – $1.45

THE GREATEST STORY EVER TOLD – Fulton Oursler (D121) – $1.45

WE AND OUR CHILDREN – Mary Reed Newland. Counsels for molding the child in Christian virtues (D123) – 95¢

LIVING FLAME OF LOVE – St. John of the Cross (Translated by E. Allison Peers) – (D129) – $1.45

A HISTORY OF PHILOSOPHY: VOLUME 1 – GREECE AND ROME (2 Parts) – Frederick Copleston, S.J. (D134a, D134b) – $1.75 ea.

A HISTORY OF PHILOSOPHY: VOLUME 2 – MEDIAEVAL PHILOSOPHY (2 Parts) – Frederick Copleston, S.J. Part I – Augustine to Bonaventure. Part II – Albert the Great to Duns Scotus (D135a, D135b) – $1.45 ea.

A HISTORY OF PHILOSOPHY: VOLUME 3 – LATE MEDIAEVAL AND RENAISSANCE PHILOSOPHY (2 Parts) – Frederick Copleston, S.J. Part I – Ockham to the Speculative Mystics. Part II – The Revival of Platonism to Suárez (D136a, D136b) – $1.45 ea.

A HISTORY OF PHILOSOPHY: VOLUME 4 – MODERN PHILOSOPHY: Descartes to Leibniz – Frederick Copleston, S.J. (D137) – $1.75

A HISTORY OF PHILOSOPHY: VOLUME 5 – MODERN PHILOSOPHY: The British Philosophers, Hobbes to Hume (2 Parts) – Frederick Copleston, S.J. Part I – Hobbes to Paley. Part II – Berkeley to Hume (D138a) – $1.45; (D138b) – $1.75

A HISTORY OF PHILOSOPHY: VOLUME 6 – MODERN PHILOSOPHY (2 Parts) – Frederick Copleston, S.J. Part I – The French Enlightenment to Kant (D139a, D139b) – $1.45 ea.

A HISTORY OF PHILOSOPHY: VOLUME 7 – MODERN PHILOSOPHY (2 Parts) – Frederick Copleston, S.J. Part I – Fichte to Hegel. Part II – Schopenhauer to Nietzsche (D140a, D140b) – $1.75 ea.

IMAGE BOOKS

A HISTORY OF PHILOSOPHY: VOLUME 8 – MODERN PHILOSOPHY: Bentham to Russell (2 Parts) – Frederick Copleston, S.J. Part I – British Empiricism and the Idealist Movement in Great Britain. Part II – Idealism in America, the Pragmatist Movement, the Revolt against Idealism (D141a, D141b) – $1.45 ea.

SEARCHING THE SCRIPTURES – John J. Dougherty (D151) – 85¢

A DOCTOR AT CALVARY – Pierre Barbet, M.D. A moving account of the Passion of our Lord (D155) – 95¢

THE SPIRITUAL EXERCISES OF ST. IGNATIUS – Translated by Anthony Mottola, Ph.D. Introduction by Robert W. Gleason, S.J. (D170) – 95¢

WE HOLD THESE TRUTHS: Catholic Reflections on the American Proposition – John Courtney Murray, S.J. (D181) – $1.25

LIFE AND HOLINESS – Thomas Merton. Exposition of the principles of the spiritual life (D183) – 85¢

MY LIFE WITH CHRIST – Anthony J. Paone, S.J. (D185) – $1.25

A FAMILY ON WHEELS: Further Adventures of the Trapp Family Singers – Maria Augusta Trapp with Ruth T. Murdoch (D187) – 85¢

AMERICAN CATHOLICISM – John Tracy Ellis. A comprehensive survey of the American Church (D190) – 95¢

THE COUNCIL, REFORM AND REUNION – with a new Introduction by Fr. Hans Kung (D198) – 95¢

WITH GOD IN RUSSIA – Walter J. Ciszek, S.J., with Daniel L. Flaherty, S.J. (D200) – $1.45

THE TWO-EDGED SWORD – John L. McKenzie, S.J. Outstanding interpretation of the Old Testament (D215) – $1.45

STRANGERS IN THE HOUSE: Catholic Youth in America – Andrew M. Greeley (D221) – 95¢

THE LILIES OF THE FIELD – William E. Barrett (D225) – 95¢

THE DIVIDING OF CHRISTENDOM – Christopher Dawson (D229) – 95¢

NO MAN IS AN ISLAND – Thomas Merton (D231) – $1.25

AND YOUNG MEN SHALL SEE VISIONS – Andrew M. Greeley. Letters to a young collegian on subjects of burning interest to young men today (D232) – 85¢

CONJECTURES OF A GUILTY BYSTANDER – Thomas Merton. A collection of notes, opinions, reflections (D234) – $1.45

THE POWER OF LOVE – Fulton J. Sheen (D235) – $1.25

IMAGE BOOKS

IMAGE BOOKS

IMAGE BOOKS

Mr. & Mrs. Don Allfande
144 W. Southern Hills
Rd.
Phoenix, Arizona

Mr. & Mrs. Jack Russell
6706 Joshua Tree
Scottsdale Lane
~~Phoenix~~, Ariz. 80253

Mr. & Mrs. Brudd Auther
3825 E Lupine
Phoenix, Ariz
85028